BURGERS

BURGERS

From Barbecue Ranch to Miso Salmon

PAUL GAYLER

PHOTOGRAPHY BY GUS FILGATE

CASTLE BOOKS

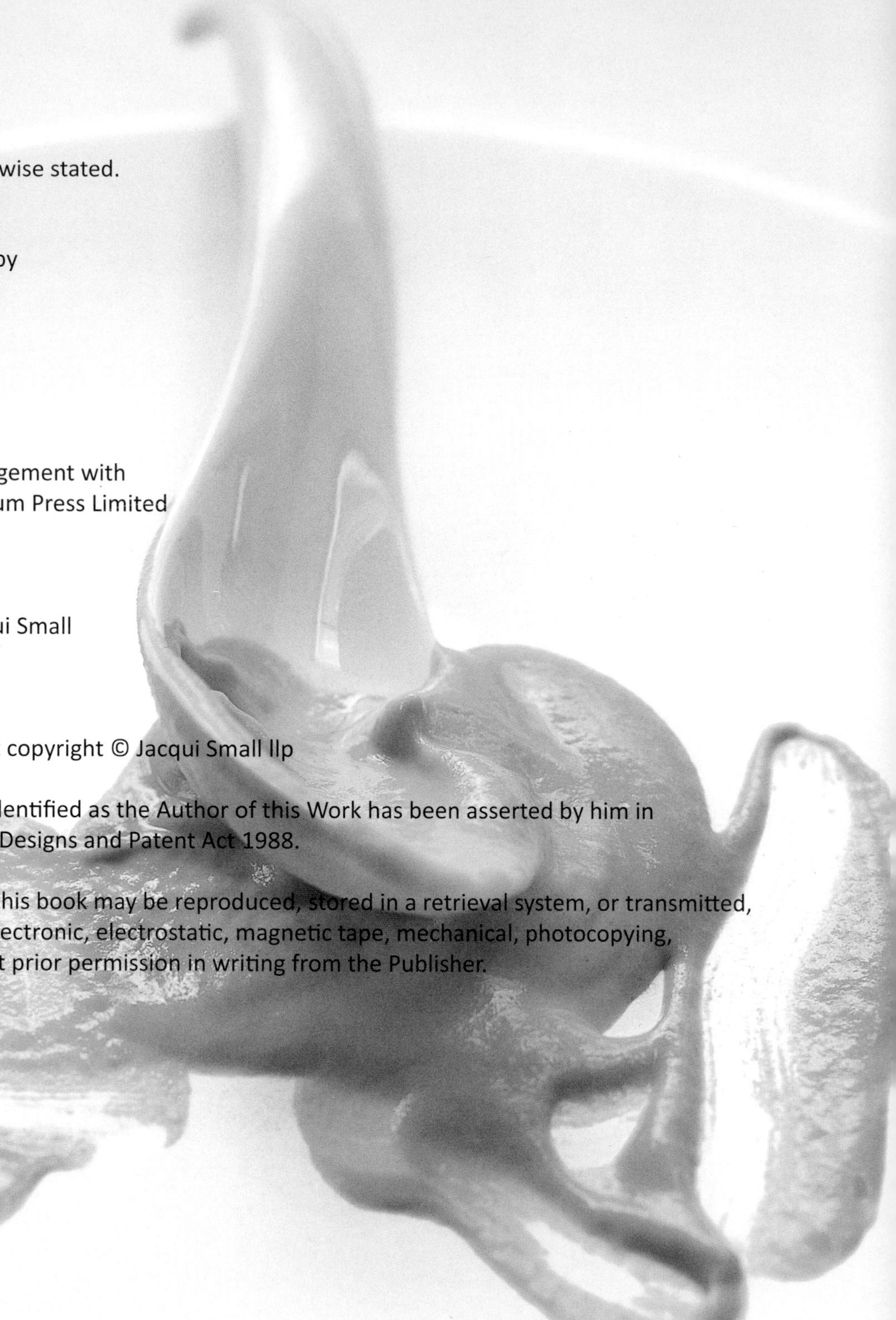

All recipes serve 4 unless otherwise stated.

This edition published in 2010 by
CASTLE BOOKS ®
a division of BOOK SALES, INC.
276 Fifth Avenue Suite 206
New York, New York 10001
USA

This edition published by arrangement with
Jacqui Small, an imprint of Aurum Press Limited
7 Greenland Street
London NW1 0ND

First published in 2004 by Jacqui Small

Publisher: Jacqui Small
Editorial Manager: Kate John
Editor: Madeline Weston
Art Director: Lawrence Morton
Food Stylist: Linda Tubby
Props Stylist: Roisin Nield
Production: Peter Colley

ISBN-13: 978-0-7858-2631-6
ISBN-10: 0-7858-2631-9

Printed and bound in China
Reprinted in 2010

Contents

You can't beat a good burger, that's why they're loved the world over. As with all brilliant ideas, the burger's appeal lies in its simplicity. What could be simpler than pressing together some good ground beef with a little seasoning, then grilling it and serving it in a bun, with pickles, ketchup, mustard, whatever takes your fancy? A well-dressed burger makes the perfect meal: nutritious and filling, with a combination of sweet/salt/sour flavors to tantalize the taste buds. What's more, it's quick to make, comforting to eat, and can be held in your hands.

The fast-food companies were quick to claim the burger as their own, but the qualities that make it suitable for mass production also make it perfect for cooking at home. So give it a go! In this book you will find over sixty recipes for burgers, ranging from the traditional beef versions such as the Classic All-American, to a Greek Souvlaki Burger, a Mediterranean Swordfish Burger and a Middle Eastern–inspired Pumpkin Couscous Burger, plus some exciting ideas for relishes and accompaniments. None of them is difficult or time consuming, and all of them will tempt you to make burgers the centerpiece of your meal, whether it's a summer barbecue, a quick midweek family supper, or a celebration dinner (Fillet Burger Rossini with Foie Gras and Truffle Glaze would be perfect). Some of the burgers are designed for serving as pre-dinner nibbles with drinks: the Thai Lobster and Lemongrass Sticks, Peking Duck Wraps, and the Trattoria Burger, but all the other burgers can be scaled down to serve in this way too.

Chefs everywhere are rediscovering the burger. I hope this book will encourage you to do the same, and to restore the burger to its rightful place at the heart of the family kitchen.

The history of the burger

For people all over the world, the hamburger has come to represent modern American culture, yet this fast-food icon has a surprisingly long history, with roots buried deep in northern Europe.

Grinding beef to make it easier to eat is not a recent idea. In medieval Russia, tribes known as Tartars used to shred beef and eat it raw, hence steak tartare. German soldiers picked up the idea in the fourteenth century and took it back to their homeland, where the meat was flavored with spices and herbs, and eaten raw or cooked. This eventually became known as Hamburg steak, after the German city, and crossed the Atlantic with German immigrants in the nineteenth century. The term *hamburger* appeared on a menu at Delmonico's restaurant in New York as early as 1834, and by the 1890s it was common across the United States. In the early days, Hamburg steak was a piece of beef that had been pounded to make it more tender, not ground, but by 1902 there were recipes in cookbooks that included instructions to grind the meat and mix it with seasonings.

The hamburger made its big leap to immortality when someone had the idea of serving it in a bun. Suddenly, it was portable, convenient and, thanks to the various toppings and the bread that soaked up the juices, ten times as delicious. The question is, who thought of it first? Several places in the United States claim to be the birthplace of the modern hamburger. Seymour, Wisconsin, has built a Hamburger Hall of Fame to back up its story that Charlie Nagreen, aged fifteen, was the first person ever to serve hamburgers, at the Outgamie County Fair in 1885. At Hamburg, New York, the legend goes that the Menches brothers substituted ground beef for pork in their famous sausage sandwiches, which they sold from a stand at a county fair there in 1885, and renamed them hamburgers. But what isn't in any doubt, since it was written up by a reporter from the *New York Tribune*, is that beef patties in a bun, called hamburgers, were on sale at the St. Louis World's Fair in 1904. It seems that the vendor was Fletcher Davis, who had already built up quite a reputation in his hometown of Athens, Texas, for his toasted steak sandwiches. The term *hamburger* became shortened to "burger", opening up the way for cheeseburgers and more modern inventions, such as tuna burgers, veggie burgers, and chicken burgers. The early twentieth century was a time of rapid change in American society. As cars became affordable and better roads were built, the population became increasingly mobile. This new freedom opened up a new way of eating, too, one that meant you didn't even have to get out of your car. Drive-in restaurants, selling barbecued meats, hamburgers and hot dogs, became popular places for young people to hang out. Two brothers, Richard and Maurice McDonald, opened their McDonald Brothers Burger Bar Drive-in in 1940. Despite its success, they became tired of their teenage customers, and decided to open a new kind of restaurant where entire families could come and eat cheaply. The only food on sale was to be burgers; paper plates, cups, and bags were to be used; and a factory production-line system in the kitchen meant that service was ultra-quick. Soon people were queuing round the block for the cheapest burgers in town, and the concept of fast food was born.

Now the hamburger is almost entirely associated with fast-food restaurants. It is the all-time American favorite, with nearly 5.5 billion burgers sold each year in the United States alone, meaning that the average American eats three a week. Yet familiarity has bred contempt. As the hamburger's popularity grew, unscrupulous operators sprang up who squeezed as much profit as they could out of inferior beef and damp, tasteless buns. From being a quick, nutritious snack, the hamburger came to symbolize for some the worst excesses of fast-food culture.

This book isn't about fast food, however. It's a celebration of what made the burger great in the first place. A well-made burger transcends the sum of its parts to become truly sublime. This is a fact that many talented chefs are aware of, which is why the burger has undergone something of a revival recently, and now appears on some of the classiest restaurant menus in America. It may be the all-American classic; it may be a chef's flight of fancy, sandwiched between two halves of a bun, a crisp baguette or a light, fluffy focaccia; tuna, lobster, lamb, venison, roasted vegetables, goat's cheese, you name it. Yet all these burgers have something in common with the original: they are made from a very few quality ingredients, cooked quickly, and served up as fresh as can be. Now more than ever, the burger offers us the kind of food we want to eat. Its timeless appeal ensures that one hundred years after its first documented appearance at the St. Louis World's Fair, the hamburger endures as not just America's but the world's most popular food.

How to make a burger

Burgers are so quick to make at home that once you get in the habit you might wonder why you ever bothered to buy them. Making them yourself means that you can control the quality of the meat and customize the flavorings to your own taste. When you've mastered the classic hamburger, move on to other meats (lamb, in particular, makes a great burger), game, fish, and seafood, even vegetables, grains, and beans. And have fun with the accompaniments—there's a big selection to choose from. Below are a few guidelines to ensure that your burgers always turn out the best:

Meat

Choosing meat: Because burgers are cooked for just a short time and contain only a few flavorings, the flavor of the meat shines through. This means that the better the meat, the better your burgers will taste. There's no need to buy expensive cuts, though. Instead, go for skirt, shin, or chuck when making beef burgers. For lamb or pork, shoulder or leg is fine. Avoid packs of ground meat, as they tend to be wet and flavorless. For a juicy, succulent burger, you need to use meat that is about 20 percent fat. This drains off during cooking but ensures that the burger remains moist, effectively basting it as it cooks. Over-lean meat can result in a dry, tough burger. Game makes excellent burgers. Meats such as pheasant and ostrich are well flavored and nutritious. Because they are so lean, add a little fat to the mixture in the form of pork.

Preparing meat: The meat should be coarsely ground, if it is too finely ground, the burger is more likely to fall apart and the texture is less satisfying. Additions, such as garlic or chilies, should be chopped very finely. Most butchers grind their meat on a fine or medium setting, so you may have to ask for it to be prepared for you. Alternatively, grind it yourself at home, trimming it first. An old-fashioned hand-cranked grinder is surprisingly satisfying to use. You could use a food processor, but it's quite hard to get the right texture with it. Chop the meat into small cubes first with a large, sharp knife, then pulse it in the machine, being careful not to let it turn into a paste.

Making the burgers: Always chill the meat well before use; this helps the ingredients cohere when you mix them together. Then combine all the ingredients as quickly and lightly as possible, otherwise the burgers will be dense and heavy. Meats such as chicken can be pulsed briefly with all the flavorings in a food processor, but for most meats, once they are ground it's best to mix everything together with your hands in a large bowl. Use wet hands to shape the burgers, so the mixture doesn't stick to them. Don't squeeze the mixture into shape; just press it lightly together until it forms a ball. Then flatten it gently with the palm of your hand and neaten the edges so they don't fray. Make sure the burgers are an even thickness (about 1 inch), so they cook evenly. Once you have shaped the burgers, place them on a baking tray, and chill again, to firm up the meat before cooking.

Fish

When you are making fish burgers, buy very fresh fish fillets, remove the skin, and check the flesh carefully for bones. Chill well. The fish is then usually finely chopped by hand and mixed with the other ingredients, or mixed to a coarse paste in a food processor, depending on the desired texture. Fish can give off liquid sometimes, especially if the recipe requires you to marinate it, so drain this off before dividing the mixture into burgers. Shape as for meat and chill until firm. Cooking fish burgers requires care, so follow the instructions on the following page.

Vegetables

Making vegetarian burgers gives you a chance to be really inventive: lentils, nuts, grains, such as millet and buckwheat, even cottage cheese and goat cheese all make fantastic burgers. The secret is to get the mixture the right consistency so it will hold together during cooking. Ground nuts, bread crumbs, and egg are all useful for binding the mixture. Mixing everything together in a blender or food processor is a quick method, and you can then shape and chill your burgers as for meat, above. Today, vegetarian burgers are not only for vegetarians!

Basic methods of cooking

There's no denying that burgers taste best when cooked on a chargrill. They must be the ultimate barbecue food, grilled over glowing coals, then slapped into a lightly toasted bun with the accompaniments of your choice, and devoured straight away. Burgers such as vegetable and fish, however, can be too delicate for the chargrill, and are better fried in a little oil. However you cook your burgers, it rarely takes more than 10 minutes. No wonder they're everyone's favorite fast food!

Barbecuing

The secret of cooking on a barbecue is to wait until the flames have died down and you are left with glowing, reddish-grey embers. This generally means lighting the barbecue at least 40 minutes before you want to start cooking. Burgers are best cooked over a medium-high heat, i. e. when the red-hot coals are covered with a layer of white ash.

When the barbecue has reached the right temperature, brush the burgers with a little oil and put them on the grill: a heavy-duty one with fairly thick bars will minimize sticking. Resist the temptation to move them about or try to turn them until they are nicely charred underneath, otherwise they will stick.

Once a crust has formed, you should be able to release the burger from the bars of the grill and flip it over with a metal spatula to brown the other side. Besides making burgers easier to turn, searing the surface in this way also makes them more appetizing, the lightly charred surface contains all those wonderful caramelized flavors that make chargrilled food so irresistible.

There's no need to press down on the burgers with a spatula to speed up cooking, if you do this, the precious juices will be lost and the burgers will be dry.

Cook the burgers according to taste: if you like them rare, test by pressing the center gently with a finger, it should feel soft and yielding. The firmer it is, the more cooked it will be. Pork and chicken should always be cooked right through.

Frying

If you find a ridged grill pan difficult, and some burgers can have a tendency to stick or break up on them, it's fine to use a frying pan instead. This method is recommended for delicate burgers such as chicken and fish. Choose a nonstick frying pan with a heavy base so it will conduct the heat evenly. Heat a thin film of oil in it until almost smoking hot (for meat burgers) or until moderately hot (for fish and vegetable burgers), then add the burgers and cook until well colored underneath. Turn with a spatula and cook the other side. Be careful not to overcrowd the pan, or the burgers will steam instead of fry. Except for tuna, which can be served rare like beef, fish burgers should be cooked all the way through, and should be golden on the outside, or at the most just lightly charred. For vegetable burgers, which are generally made from pre-cooked ingredients, all you need to do is ensure that they form a good golden crust on the outside and heat through thoroughly in the center. A couple of the vegetable burgers in this book are deep-fried. Immersing them in hot oil like this gives them a wonderful, crisp crust and a contrasting soft center. Heat the oil to 350°F in a deep-fat fryer or a deep saucepan and fry the burgers a few at a time. Drain on kitchen paper to remove excess fat before serving.

Grilling and broiling

For grilling burgers indoors, a ridged cast-iron grill pan is invaluable. Not only does it give food a hint of the smoky flavor that you get on an outdoor barbecue but the ridges mean that the fat drains away, making it a healthy cooking method. Choose a large one that goes across two rings on your hob, so you can cook a decent batch of burgers in one go. Before cooking, leave the grill pan over a medium-high heat until it is almost smoking hot (a good way of testing it is to throw a drop or two of water onto it; if it sizzles, the pan is hot enough). Then brush the burgers lightly with oil and proceed as above.

You can also cook burgers under a broiler, although – because they don't have direct contact with the heat – they will lack that wonderful smoky flavor.

The ultimate burger with 'the works'

CLASSIC BEEF

The ultimate burger with 'the works'

1 lb 12 oz good quality, coarsely ground
  beef, chilled
½ onion, finely chopped
½ garlic clove, crushed
1 tbsp chopped fresh flat-leaf parsley
½ tsp Dijon mustard
½ tbsp Worcestershire sauce
1 egg yolk
salt and freshly ground black pepper
vegetable or sunflower oil for cooking

1 Place the chilled meat in a large bowl; add the onion, garlic, parsley, mustard, and Worcestershire sauce.
2 Add the egg yolk and seasoning, and mix thoroughly. Leave in the refrigerator for 1 hour.
3 Using wet hands, shape into 4 evenly sized burgers.
4 Heat a chargrill or pan grill until smoking hot.
5 Brush the burgers with a little oil, place on the grill and cook for 3–4 minutes on each side, until well browned, but still pink in the center.
6 Serve the burgers in the toasted buns, spread and garnished with your choice of 'the works'.

TO SERVE • 4 BURGER BUNS, HALVED, TOASTED

'THE WORKS' • HORSERADISH AND SOUR CREAM CHIVE SAUCE
• TABASCO–CUMIN KETCHUP (SEE PAGE 125) • SWEET PICKLED DILL GHERKINS
• DICED AVOCADO • RED ONION RINGS • DIJON MUSTARD AIOLI

Horseradish and sour cream chive sauce
½ cup sour cream
1 tbsp creamed horseradish
  relish
1 tbsp chopped fresh chives
• Whisk the ingredients together and serve.

Dijon mustard aioli
½ cup aioli (see page 126)
1 tsp Dijon mustard
salt and freshly ground black
  pepper
• Whisk the ingredients together and serve.

Classic all-American burger

1 lb 12 oz well-trimmed, coarsely ground
  beef, chilled
1 onion, finely chopped
salt and freshly ground black pepper
vegetable or sunflower oil for cooking
8 slices American-style cheese
1 cup shredded iceberg lettuce leaves
2 large tomatoes, thickly sliced
1 onion, sliced

1 Mix the meat and the onion in a large bowl, season with salt, plenty of black pepper, and chill for 1 hour.
2 Divide the mix into 4 x 7 oz evenly sized burgers, and brush liberally all over with the oil.
3 Heat a chargrill or pan grill until very hot, add the burgers and cook for 3–4 minutes on each side, until cooked and slightly charred all over.
4 Preheat the broiler to its highest setting.
5 Place the burgers on a broiler rack and cover with the cheese slices, and broil until melted.
6 Toast the buns, brush the bases with mustard, and the lids with the mayonnaise.
7 Top the base of the buns with the shredded iceberg, followed by a burger, then by the onion and tomato slices. Finally, top with the sliced dill pickles, and replace the bun lids.
8 Serve with the ultimate fries, and lots of tomato ketchup.

TO SERVE • 4 BURGER BUNS, SPLIT • ¼ CUP MILD AMERICAN MUSTARD • ¼ CUP GOOD QUALITY MAYONNAISE • 2 SWEET DILL PICKLES, SLICED
• THE ULTIMATE FRIES (SEE PAGE 139) • SIMPLE TOMATO KETCHUP (SEE PAGE 125), OR STORE BOUGHT

Blackened burger with grilled onion salad and yellow pico de gallo

Traditional Cajun-style burgers from the Deep South are always preferred well dressed and well seasoned; here they are unusually served on a warm French baguette, which I think is delicious. Although not normally served with a pico de gallo, I love this Mexican-style relish, it is cool and offsets the spicy burger beautifully.

vegetable or sunflower oil for cooking
1 onion
1 garlic clove, crushed
5 oz smoked sausage of your choice, such as chorizo, cut into ¼ inch dice
1 lb 4 oz well-trimmed, coarsely ground beef
¼ tsp dried thyme
¼ tsp dried oregano
¼ tsp ground cumin
⅛ tsp chili powder
salt and freshly ground black pepper

1 Heat a small frying pan, and add a thin film of the oil to the pan; add the onion, garlic, and sausage and fry until softened and lightly golden. Transfer to a large bowl, and allow to cool.
2 Add the ground beef, dried herbs, and spices, and mix together thoroughly; season with salt and pepper and chill for 1 hour.
3 Divide into 4 evenly sized burgers, and brush liberally with the oil.
4 Heat a chargrill or pan grill until very hot and add the burgers. Cook for 3–4 minutes on each side or longer if you prefer.
5 Halve the baguette, dress the bases with a spread of chili mayo, topped with shredded iceberg lettuce. Top with the grilled onion salad, a burger, and finally a good spoonful of the yellow pico de gallo.
6 Close the burgers and serve.

Grilled onion salad

1 large or 2 small red onions,
  unpeeled
½ cup olive oil
2 tbsp roughly chopped fresh
  cilantro
juice of ½ lemon
splash of balsamic vinegar
salt and freshly ground black
  pepper

• Cut the onion across into 4 thick
slices, about ¾ inch thick, keeping
the skins on each slice.
• Heat a chargrill or pan grill until
hot. Brush the onion slices liberally
all over both sides with half the oil.
• Place the onions on the grill and
cook until almost charred brown,
but not burnt. Brush with more oil
during cooking if needed.
• Carefully using a fish slice,
remove the onions from the grill
and transfer to a shallow tray.
Discard the outer skin.
• Mix the remaining oil, chopped
cilantro, lemon juice, and a splash
of balsamic vinegar in a bowl, and
brush over the warm onions;
season to taste and keep warm.

TO SERVE • 4 X 5-INCH LENGTHS WARM BAGUETTE OR BUNS • CHILI MAYO (SEE PAGE 126)
• 1 CUP SHREDDED ICEBURG LETTUCE • GRILLED ONION SALAD • YELLOW PICO DE GALLO (SEE PAGE 128)

Open-faced Roquefort burger

½ cup crumbled Roquefort cheese

scant 1 cup unsalted butter, softened

2 tbsp snipped fresh chives

1 lb 10 oz good quality, coarsely ground beef, well chilled

1 onion, finely chopped

1 tsp Dijon mustard

1 tsp Worcestershire sauce

2 egg yolks

1 garlic clove, crushed

salt and freshly ground black pepper

vegetable or sunflower oil for cooking

1 In a bowl, mix together the cheese with the butter and snipped chives.

2 Cut a sheet of waxed paper approximately 10 x 10 inches. Mold the prepared butter in a strip about 1½ inches wide along the front edge of the paper then roll up tightly, twisting the ends to form a fat bonbon shape. Place in the freezer overnight.

3 In a large bowl, mix the remaining ingredients, then divide the hamburger mix into 8 evenly sized patties.

4 Remove the cheese roll from the freezer, allow to soften slightly and cut into 4 equal slices.

5 Place a slice of cheese roll on 4 of the patties and use the remaining 4 patties as lids; with your fingertips, pinch the edges together to seal in the cheese filling. Brush the burgers with a little oil.

6 Heat the grill and, when smoking hot, cook the burgers for 4–5 minutes on each side.

7 To serve, top each section of the baguette with a sliced tomato, then a grilled burger, and top with some dressed salad leaves, and serve.

TO SERVE · 4 X 5-INCH LENGTHS FRENCH BAGUETTE · 8 TOMATOES, SLICED · 1 CUP ARUGULA LEAVES · ¼ CUP FRENCH DRESSING OF YOUR CHOICE

Bymark hamburger
Sirloin burger with porcini mushrooms, Brie de Meaux and truffle aioli

This wonderful recipe comes courtesy of top Canadian chef Mark McEwan, of Toronto's trendy North 44 Restaurant. The melting Brie and fat juicy porcini mushrooms work brilliantly together while the truffle aioli adds a touch of elegance.

1 lb 12 oz trimmed beef striploin, hand chopped

salt and freshly ground black pepper

olive oil for cooking

4 fresh porcini mushrooms, sliced ½ inch thick

4 slices Brie de Meaux cheese

Truffle aioli
½ cup good quality mayonnaise

1 tbsp lemon juice

2 tsp truffle oil or paste

· Whisk the ingredients together and serve.

1 Place the chopped striploin in a bowl, season liberally with salt and pepper.
2 Form into 1-inch-thick patties, then brush lightly with olive oil.
3 Heat a chargrill or pan grill until very hot, add the burgers and grill until desired doneness (about 4 minutes per side for rare), remove.
4 Brush the sliced porcini mushrooms with the olive oil, and grill until tender, season with salt and pepper.
5 Finally, grill the buns until golden.
6 Top each burger with a slice of Brie de Meaux cheese.
7 Place the mushrooms on each burger bun base, then top with the burger and cheese slice.
8 Finally spoon over a little truffle aioli, close the burger with its lid and serve.

TO SERVE · 4 BURGER BUNS, SPLIT · TRUFFLE AIOLI

Plowman's burger with two cheeses, balsamic onion pickle, and classic coleslaw

1 tbsp unsalted butter

1 onion, finely chopped

1 garlic clove, crushed

½ tsp smoked paprika

1 tsp picked fresh thyme leaves

1 lb 12 oz well-trimmed, coarsely ground beef, chilled

2 tbsp barbecue sauce

2 tbsp chopped fresh flat-leaf parsley

2 egg yolks

salt and freshly ground black pepper

⅓ cup grated Cheddar cheese

vegetable or sunflower oil for cooking

1 Heat the butter in a frying pan, add the onion, garlic, smoked paprika, and thyme. Cook for 1–2 minutes until the onions are softened but not colored. Place in a bowl to cool.

2 Add the chilled meat, barbecue sauce, parsley, and egg yolks, and season to taste. Carefully bring the mix together, making sure not to overwork it or it will become tough. Chill in the refrigerator for 1 hour.

3 Divide the mix into 4 x 7 oz evenly sized burgers.

4 With a wet thumb, make an indent into the top of each burger. Fill the indent in each burger with Cheddar cheese then fold up the side to secure the cheese in the center. Brush liberally with the oil.

5 Heat a chargrill or pan grill until very hot, add the burgers, and cook for 3–4 minutes on each side or longer if you prefer.

6 Place a good dollop of the onion pickle on the base of each roll, then top with a slice of Emmental cheese and some sliced tomatoes.

7 Place the burger on top, followed by the coleslaw. Replace the lid and serve with the shredded iceberg lettuce and extra pickle. Jacket potatoes oozing with lots of butter would be great too!

TO SERVE · 4 LARGE CRUSTY ROLLS OR CIABATTAS, SPLIT · 4 SLICES EMMENTAL CHEESE · 2 LARGE TOMATOES, THINLY SLICED · CLASSIC COLESLAW (SEE PAGE 133) · 1 CUP SHREDDED ICEBERG LETTUCE · BALSAMIC ONION PICKLE (SEE PAGE 130)

Bloody Mary burger with celeriac Waldorf and Tabasco–cumin ketchup

1 lb 12 oz well-trimmed, coarsely ground beef
1 onion, peeled, finely chopped
1 stalk celery, peeled, finely chopped
2 tbsp tomato ketchup
1 tbsp horseradish relish
1 tbsp Worcestershire sauce
1 tbsp chopped fresh flat-leaf parsley
salt and freshly ground black pepper
vegetable or sunflower oil for cooking

1 Place the meat in a large bowl and add the onion, celery, ketchup, horseradish, Worcestershire sauce, and parsley. Season with salt and pepper. Mix well but do not overwork, then chill for 1 hour.
2 Divide the mix into 4 evenly sized burgers and brush liberally with oil.
3 Heat a chargrill or pan grill until hot, add the burgers, and cook for 5–6 minutes.
4 Toast the buns, top with shredded romaine lettuce, then a heap of celeriac Waldorf.
5 Place a burger on top, and drizzle some Tabasco–cumin ketchup over; close the bun.
6 Serve with some extra ketchup alongside and oven cheese fries. A tall glass of Bloody Mary served alongside is a welcome addition.

Celeriac Waldorf

1 celeriac, peeled
1 Granny Smith apple, peeled and cored
⅓ cup good quality crème fraîche
½ tsp Dijon mustard
2 tbsp soaked raisins
salt and freshly ground black pepper

• Cut the celeriac and apple into small matchstick-size pieces, either by hand or with a kitchen mandolin.
• Place in a bowl, add the crème fraîche, mustard and raisins; mix well and season to taste.

TO SERVE • 4 SESAME BURGER BUNS, SPLIT • ROMAINE LETTUCE LEAVES, SHREDDED
• CELERIAC WALDORF • TABASCO–CUMIN KETCHUP (SEE PAGE 125) • OVEN CHEESE FRIES (SEE PAGE 139)

New Mexican burger with smoky guacamole amd sweet potato mole

In this Mexican-inspired burger I replace the soft bun with a crispy fried corn tortilla shell that adds an interesting contrast of texture.

1 lb 6 oz good quality, coarsely ground beef, chilled
1 onion, finely chopped
2 garlic cloves, crushed
2 small red chilies, deeseeded, finely chopped
1 tsp smoked paprika
1 tsp ground cumin
3 tbsp chopped fresh cilantro
salt

1 In a large bowl, mix all the ingredients together and chill for up to 1 hour. Shape into 4 evenly sized burgers, brush with oil and grill, or fry in a nonstick pan over moderate heat, for 4–5 minutes each side, until cooked.

2 To serve, arrange 4 tortilla shells on individual serving plates, place a few salad leaves on each shell, and top with a dollop of sweet potato mole.

3 Arrange a burger on top and spoon the smoky guacamole over. Garnish with a dollop of sour cream and some cilantro leaves and serve with lime wedges.

Sweet potato mole

1 cup canned tomatoes, chopped
1 red bell pepper, deseeded, chopped
1 onion, finely chopped
1 garlic clove, crushed
1 tbsp brown sugar
1 corn tortilla, chopped
1 tbsp hot Mexican pepper sauce
1 tbsp sesame seeds, toasted
⅛ tsp each ground cinnamon, ground cumin, ground coriander, and ground cloves
1 tbsp each chopped fresh oregano and cilantro
½ cup peanut butter
1 orange sweet potato, peeled, cut into ½-inch cubes
salt and freshly ground black pepper

• Place the chopped tomatoes, red bell pepper, onion, garlic, brown sugar, tortilla, pepper sauce, sesame seeds, and herbs and spices in a saucepan, cover with ⅔ cup water, bring to a boil over a high heat.
• Cook for 10 minutes; reduce the heat, and simmer for a further 30 minutes or until the mixture is thick and aromatic.
• Place in a blender and mix to a smooth purée. Return to the pan.
• Add the peanut butter and heat, stirring, until smooth.
• Add the cubed sweet potato and cook for 10–15 minutes until the potato is just cooked; adjust the seasoning before serving.

TO SERVE • 4 CRISPY FRIED CORN TORTILLAS • GREEN SALAD LEAVES • SWEET POTATO MOLE • SMOKY GUACAMOLE • ⅓ CUP SOUR CREAM • FRESH CILANTRO LEAVES • 1 LIME CUT INTO WEDGES

Smoky guacamole

1 ripe but firm avocado, peeled, pitted
¼ cup olive oil
4 ripe but firm tomatoes, cut into
 ¼-inch dice
½ red onion, chopped
2 scallions, chopped
1 green jalepeño chili, deseeded, finely
 chopped
juice of 1 lime
pinch of sugar, pinch of ground cumin
3 tbsp chopped fresh cilantro
salt and freshly ground black pepper

• Heat a chargrill or pan grill until hot.
• Brush the avocado halves all over liberally with 1 tbsp of the oil; place on the grill and cook until lightly golden but not charred (which will make the flavor bitter), remove and allow to cool.
• Place the avocado in a bowl and mash lightly with a fork; add the tomatoes, red onion, scallions, and chili.
• Add the lime juice, sugar, ground cumin, and cilantro, and lastly the remaining oil. Adjust the seasoning and set aside.

Steak tartare burger with herb-mustard and blue-cheese aioli, and matchstick fries

1 lb 12 oz well-trimmed, coarsely ground beef, chilled
2 small shallots, finely chopped
2 tbsp chopped fresh parsley
6 cocktail gherkins, rinsed, dried, finely chopped
2 tbsp superfine capers, rinsed, finely chopped
2 egg yolks
salt and freshly ground black pepper
vegetable or sunflower oil for cooking

1 Place the meat in a large bowl, add the shallots, parsley, gherkins, and capers. Beat in the egg yolks, and season with salt and pepper; do not overwork the mix.
2 Leave in the refrigerator for 1 hour before use.
3 Divide the mix, using wet hands, into 4 x 7 oz evenly sized burgers.
4 Heat a chargrill or pan grill until very hot. Brush the burgers liberally all over with the oil.
5 Place on the grill, and cook for 3–4 minutes on each side until cooked.
6 Toast the burger buns; cover the bases with the sliced tomatoes, watercress, then the burgers.
7 Spoon the herb-mustard and blue-cheese aioli over, and cover with the top lid.
8 Serve with matchstick fries.

Herb-mustard and blue-cheese aioli

2 tbsp herb mustard
½ cup basic mayonnaise (see page 126)
1 garlic clove, crushed
2 tbsp chopped fresh chives
¾ cup of your favorite blue cheese (e.g. Stilton, Gorgonzola, Roquefort), crumbled
salt and freshly ground black pepper
• In a bowl, blend together the mustard, mayonnaise, garlic, and chives; fold in the crumbled cheese, blend well and season to taste.

TO SERVE • 4 BURGER BUNS, SPLIT • 2 BEEF TOMATOES, THINLY SLICED • 2 CUPS WATERCRESS • HERB-MUSTARD AND BLUE-CHEESE AIOLI • MATCHSTICK FRIES (SEE PAGE 139)

Barbecued oyster burger with blue-cheese sauce, and bacon, spinach, and red onion salad

1 lb 8 oz well-trimmed, coarsely ground beef, chilled
1 onion, finely chopped
1 tbsp chopped fresh flat-leaf parsley
1 tbsp horseradish relish
1 tsp tomato ketchup
1 egg, lightly beaten
salt and freshly ground black pepper
4 large freshly shucked oysters
vegetable or sunflower oil for cooking

1 Place the beef in a bowl, add the onion and parsley, and mix well. Add the horseradish, ketchup, and egg, and mix well together; season to taste. Cover, then refrigerate for 1 hour. Using wet hands, divide the mix into 4 evenly sized portions.

2 Shape each into a ball then, with wet fingers, make a deep indentation into the ball. Place 1 oyster into the hole, then seal up again to secure the oyster within. Flatten slightly into burgers, then brush liberally with oil and cook for 3–4 minutes each side, or a little longer if preferred.

3 Toast the brioche slices, top with the bacon, spinach, and red onion salad, then top with the burgers. Drizzle the blue-cheese sauce over; serve with sweet-potato fries.

Blue-cheese sauce

⅓ cup heavy cream
1 tsp fresh thyme leaves
¼ cup chicken stock
1 tsp cornstarch
½ cup crumbled blue cheese
salt and freshly ground black pepper

• In a pan, place the cream, thyme, chicken stock, and cornstarch. Over a low heat, cook for 2 minutes; remove and allow to cool slightly.
• Add the blue cheese and blend until melted. Season to taste and serve warm.

TO SERVE · 4 SLICES BRIOCHE LOAF · BACON, SPINACH, AND RED ONION SALAD (SEE PAGE 133) · BLUE-CHEESE SAUCE · SWEET-POTATO FRIES (SEE PAGE 140)

Barbecue ranch burger

with smoky corn relish and chimichurri bell peppers

5 oz cooked red kidney beans
  (canned are fine)
1 lb 8 oz trimmed, coarsely ground beef
1 onion, finely chopped
1 garlic clove, crushed
1 tsp fresh thyme leaves
1 tsp Dijon mustard
¼ cup barbecue sauce (see page 125)
salt and freshly ground black pepper
vegetable or sunflower oil for cooking
4 wooden skewers

TO SERVE • 4 CHORIZO BURGER BUNS, SPLIT (SEE PAGE 135)
• CHIMICHURRI BELL PEPPERS (SEE PAGE 129) • SMOKY CORN RELISH
(SEE PAGE 112) • SPICY RED-CHILI ONION RINGS (SEE PAGE 140)

1 Place the beans in a bowl and crush them with a fork.
2 Add the remaining ingredients, except the oil, and work together to form a paste; do not overwork. Chill for 1 hour in the refrigerator.
3 Divide the mix into 4 evenly sized burgers and brush liberally with the oil.
4 Heat a chargrill or pan grill until hot, add the burgers and cook for 4–5 minutes until cooked.
5 Toast the buns; place the chimichurri bell peppers on the base buns, top each with a burger, and add a dollop of corn relish on top. Close with the top of the buns.
6 Plunge a wooden skewer down through the center of each burger bun, place the onion rings draped over the sticks, and serve.

Barbecued hamburgers for a crowd (makes 32)

Eula Mae Doré has been cooking her Cajun specialities on Avery Island, Louisiana, for almost half a century. This recipe is for those not lucky enough to visit the Island to sample her home cooking! The Island has also been home to Tabasco sauce since 1868.

6 lb ground beef
2 lb lean ground pork
½ cup freshly chopped yellow onions
1½ tbsp salt
1 tbsp cayenne
1 tbsp freshly ground black pepper
1 tbsp Tabasco sauce
2 tbsp Worcestershire sauce
½ cup vegetable oil

1 Combine all the ingredients except the oil in a very large mixing bowl; mix well. Form into about 32 evenly sized patties and brush with the oil.
2 Heat a chargrill, pan grill or frying pan, and grill or fry to desired doneness.
3 More oil can be brushed on the patties while they cook.
4 Just before taking the patties off the heat, brush them liberally with Beb's barbecue sauce. Toast the small burger buns, place the burgers in them, and serve.

TO SERVE • 32 SMALL BURGER BUNS
• 1¾ CUPS BEB'S BARBECUE SAUCE (SEE PAGE 125)

Big Apple deli burger with Swiss cheese, and barbecue coleslaw

scant ½ cup tomato juice
2 shallots, finely chopped
1 tbsp coriander seeds, toasted, crushed
¼ tsp cayenne pepper
½ tsp paprika
1 tbsp molasses
1 lb 12 oz well-trimmed, coarsely ground beef, chilled
1 tbsp chopped fresh flat-leaf parsley
salt and freshly ground black pepper

1 Place the tomato juice, shallots, spices, and molasses in a small pan and bring to a boil; cook for 1 minute, then remove and allow to cool.

2 Place the meat and parsley in a bowl, add the cooked sauce, and mix well. Cover and place in the refrigerator for up to 1 hour.

3 Divide the mix into 4 evenly sized burgers, and brush liberally with oil.

4 Heat a chargrill or pan grill until very hot. Place the burgers on the grill and cook for 3–4 minutes on each side.

5 Toast the buns, then lightly spread the base buns with mustard.

6 Top with a burger and a slice of Gruyère cheese, place under a hot grill to melt. Top with some sliced gherkin and the lettuce. Garnish with the barbecue coleslaw and serve. Baked jacket potatoes go particularly well with this burger.

TO SERVE · 4 RYE OR PLAIN BURGER BUNS, SPLIT · MUSTARD · 4 LETTUCE LEAVES · 2 DILL PICKLES, THINLY SLICED · 4 SLICES SWISS GRUYÈRE CHEESE · BARBECUE COLESLAW (SEE PAGE 133)

The Wolseley hamburger

Since the Wolseley restaurant opened its doors in autumn 2003, it has received many accolades for its simple, big-flavored and down-to-earth cooking. Chef Chris Galvin, a great friend, is the main reason for its rapid rise to fame.

1 lb 6 oz lean chuck steak, coarsely ground, chilled

5½ oz beef fat, preferably from striploin, finely ground

salt and freshly ground black pepper

vegetable or sunflower oil for cooking

1 Place the steak and beef fat in a bowl along with a little seasoning. Bring the mix together, forming it lightly, just enough to hold. Do not overwork or the mix will become tough. Chill in the refrigerator for 1 hour before use.

2 Heat a chargrill or pan grill until very hot.

3 Divide the mix into 4 evenly sized burgers and brush liberally with oil.

4 Cook until desired degree, according to personal taste.

5 Toast the buns on the grill. Place the burgers on the bun bases, add a slice of onion, slice of tomato, and finally slices of dill pickles. Top with the lid and serve.

Fritas with Cuban avocado salsa and tomato sofrito

Fritas is the name of mini-sized hamburgers, eaten on the go all over Cuba. They are sold by street vendors and they make the ideal snack food. I like to serve these burgers with spicy plantain chips, known affectionately as chili willies! Allow two burgers per person.

2 cups fresh white bread crumbs
½ cup milk
1 lb 5 oz well-trimmed, coarsely ground
  beef
7 oz ground pork
1 egg, lightly beaten
1 onion, peeled, finely chopped
1 garlic clove, crushed
1 tbsp light soy sauce
2 tsp tomato ketchup
1 tsp Worcestershire sauce
pinch of paprika
salt and freshly ground black pepper
vegetable or sunflower oil for cooking

1 Soak the bread crumbs in the milk for 5 minutes, or until all the liquid is absorbed. In a bowl gently combine both meats with the bread crumbs. Add all the remaining ingredients, mix well together but do not overwork. Place in the refrigerator for 1 hour.
2 Divide the mix into 8 small, evenly sized burgers, brush liberally with the oil.
3 Heat a chargrill or pan grill until very hot, add the burgers and cook for 2–3 minutes on each side, or longer if preferred.
4 Toast the buns; top the bases with the shredded iceberg, followed by the salsa. Top each with a burger, then spoon some hot tomato sofrito over.
5 Replace the burger lids, serve with the spicy plantain chips, and enjoy!

TO SERVE · 8 SMALL BURGER BUNS, SPLIT · 1 CUP SHREDDED ICEBERG LETTUCE · CUBAN AVOCADO SALSA (SEE PAGE 131) · TOMATO SOFRITO · SPICY PLANTAIN CHIPS (SEE PAGE 140)

Tomato sofrito

2 tbsp olive oil
1 onion, peeled, finely chopped
2 garlic cloves, crushed
½ tsp dried oregano
½ tsp ground cumin
2 tbsp hot pepper sauce
14 oz canned peeled plum tomatoes or 1 lb fresh tomatoes, chopped
1 tbsp tomato purée

• Heat the olive oil in a pan, add the onion, garlic, and dried oregano; cook over a low heat for 5–6 minutes until softened.
• Add the cumin, hot pepper sauce and cook for a further 2 minutes.
• Add the chopped tomatoes, tomato purée, and cook for 10–15 minutes until all the juices have evaporated and the sofrito is thick in consistency. This will keep, covered, in the refrigerator for 2 weeks.

Rumpsteak burger with bacon brioche, and snail and parsley butter sauce

Richard Corrigan , chef-proprietor and talented chef of the Lindsay House in London has been cooking wonderful, inventive dishes like this for many years—to rave reviews.

1 lb 5 oz well-trimmed rump steak, chilled
⅓ cup beef bone marrow
1 tbsp unsalted butter
1 small onion, peeled, finely chopped
2 tsp chopped fresh marjoram leaves
salt and freshly ground black pepper
sunflower oil for cooking

1 Preheat the oven to 450°F.

2 Using a sharp knife, chop the meat until it has a very fine ground texture. Place in a bowl; grate the bone marrow directly into the bowl.

3 Heat the butter in a small pan and sweat the onion and marjoram until soft but not colored. Cool slightly, then add to the meat in the bowl; season well.

4 Mix together with your hands without squeezing, then divide into 4 and shape each portion lightly into a thick patty, like a tournedos, about 1 inch thick. Do not press together or the steak burgers will be tough.

5 Heat a film of oil in a frying pan with an ovenproof handle.

6 Sear and brown the burgers gently on both sides, then transfer the pan to the oven and finish cooking—3 minutes for rare, 5 minutes for medium rare. Toast the brioche slices under a preheated grill.

7 Set each steak burger on a slice of brioche, and serve the snail and parsley butter sauce alongside, with the crispy potatoes cooked in duck fat.

TO SERVE · 4 SLICES BACON BRIOCHE (SEE PAGE 136) · CRISPY POTATOES COOKED IN DUCK FAT
· SNAIL AND PARSLEY BUTTER SAUCE

Snail and parsley butter sauce

2 tbsp olive oil
6 oz canned snails, drained, roughly chopped
1 garlic clove, crushed
3 egg yolks
⅔ cup good quality French unsalted butter, clarified
¼ cup roughly chopped fresh flat-leaf parsley
salt and freshly ground black pepper
cayenne pepper
1 tsp lemon juice

· Heat a small frying pan with the oil until hot, add the snails and garlic, and sauté for 2 minutes until lightly golden in color; remove, keep warm.

· Place the egg yolks along with 1 tbsp of water in a heatproof bowl, and place above a pan of simmering water.

· Whisk vigorously until the egg thickens in volume and becomes light and fluffy. Remove the bowl from the pan, then gradually add the clarified butter to the eggs in a thin stream, until the mixture thickens (do not add too much butter at one go, or the mix will separate).

· When all the butter has been added, the mixture should be thick enough to coat the back of a spoon.

· Carefully add the snails and the parsley, season with salt and pepper, a little cayenne, and lemon juice; keep warm.

Crispy potatoes cooked in duck fat

4 medium-large baking potatoes, washed
¼ cup sunflower oil
2 tbsp duck fat, canned or rendered
coarse sea salt

• Preheat the oven to 350°F.
• Place the potatoes on a baking tray and place in the preheated oven to cook for 1 hour; remove and cool slightly, cut in half lengthwise.
• Using a large tablespoon, carefully remove the inner part, leaving the skin behind and keeping the inside of the potato intact.
• Cut the potatoes into thick wedges lengthwise.
• Heat the oil and fat in a large nonstick frying pan, add the potatoes, and cook until golden and crispy, turning them often for even coloring.
• Drain on kitchen paper; sprinkle with sea salt before serving.

Spiced Mediterranean burgers (serves 8)

British television celebrity chef and good friend Anthony Worrall Thompson is renowned for his passion for Mediterranean cuisine. This burger encapsulates it all—it is full of flavor, delicately spiced, and wonderful cooked over a barbecue.

1 lb finely ground beef
1 lb finely ground lamb
½ onion, peeled, finely grated
1 tsp finely chopped garlic
1 tbsp extra-virgin olive oil
2 tbsp chopped fresh flat-leaf parsley
1 tbsp chopped fresh cilantro
1 tsp dried oregano
½ tsp ground cinnamon
½ tsp ground cumin
1 tsp hot pepper sauce
salt and freshly ground black pepper

1 Preheat the barbecue or broiler.
2 Place the burger ingredients in a large bowl, blend the mixture with your hands, taking care not to overwork it.
3 Form the mixture into 8 long oval shapes, about 1 inch thick.
4 Chargrill, broil, or fry the burgers for about 5 minutes on each side for rare, or to your taste.
5 Split the rolls or pita breads without cutting them through. Remove some of the bread from the center of the rolls. Place some tomato and shallot slices in the rolls, add the burgers, and garnish with flat-leaf parsley, fresh cilantro, and Greek-style yogurt.

TO SERVE · 8 SMALL BAGUETTE ROLLS/PITA BREAD · 8 SHALLOTS, PEELED, THINLY SLICED · CHOPPED FRESH FLAT-LEAF PARSLEY · 4 LARGE TOMATOES, THINLY SLICED · 4 WHOLE FRESH CILANTRO LEAVES · ⅔ CUP PLAIN GREEK-STYLE YOGURT

Beet burger

This Scandinavian-style burger recipe from friend Jill Dupleix is both tasty and unusual. A self-taught cook, Jill became *The Times* cook in 2000, and is one of Britain's best-loved and respected food writers. This recipe comes from her book *Simple Food*.

1 tbsp unsalted butter
1 tbsp olive oil
1 onion, peeled, finely chopped
1 lb ground beef
2 egg yolks
1 tbsp capers, rinsed and chopped
sea salt and freshly ground black pepper
3 tbsp pickled beets, finely chopped
1 tbsp pickled beet juice
vegetable oil for cooking

1 Heat the butter and olive oil in a frying pan, and cook the onion slowly until pale and soft, then allow to cool.
2 Combine the ground beef, egg yolks, capers, sea salt, and pepper.
3 Add the onion and mix thoroughly together.
4 Add the pickled beets and juice, mix well.
5 With wet hands, shape the mixture into 4 large flat burgers (the traditional shape), or make 8 smaller, taller patties.
6 Heat a chargrill or cast iron grill pan, oil it and the burgers lightly, and cook them on a medium heat for about 5 minutes each side (alternatively heat a little oil in a frying pan and fry them).
7 Toast the muffins; serve the burgers on the toasted muffins with a little salad of tossed green leaves, or a little wilted spinach and small boiled new potatoes.

TO SERVE · 4 ENGLISH MUFFINS · SALAD OF TOSSED GREEN LEAVES OR WILTED SPINACH · SMALL BOILED NEW POTATOES

TO SERVE • 4 BURGER BUNS OR ENGLISH MUFFINS, SPLIT • CELERIAC RÉMOULADE (SEE PAGE 133) • 1 CUP WATERCRESS • 3 OZ FOIE GRAS, IN 4 SLICES • 8 SLICES FRESH OR PRESERVED TRUFFLE (OPTIONAL) • TRUFFLE GLAZE • MIXED LEAF SALAD • THE ULTIMATE FRIES (SEE PAGE 139)

Truffle glaze
1 tbsp honey
⅔ cup medium sweet
  Madeira wine
1 tbsp Champagne vinegar
⅓ cup olive oil
1 tbsp truffle oil or truffle
  paste
salt and freshly ground
  black pepper
• Place the honey and
Madeira in a small pan, bring
to a boil.
• Reduce the liquid down
until only 2 tbsp remain.
• Add the vinegar, then whisk
in the oils to form an
emulsion; season to taste.

Fillet burger rossini with foie gras, truffle glaze, and celeriac rémoulade

This is a bit of a 'posh' burger! The ingredients may be more luxurious than most burger recipes, but it's a burger I would happily enjoy every day. You have to spoil yourself occasionally!

14 oz well-trimmed, coarsely ground beef, chilled
½ tbsp picked thyme leaves
salt and freshly ground black pepper
vegetable or sunflower oil for cooking
4 x 4 oz fillet steaks

1 Mix the ground beef, thyme, and seasoning in a bowl, cover and chill for 1 hour. Divide the mix into 4 small evenly sized burgers, brush liberally with oil.

2 Heat a chargrill or pan grill until very hot, add the burgers and small fillet steaks, and cook for 2–3 minutes on each side.

3 Toast the buns; place a good dollop of celeriac rémoulade on the bun bases, then top with the grilled fillet steaks, a little watercress, followed by the burgers. Heat a nonstick pan with no oil and, when very hot, sauté the foie gras for 30 seconds each side.

4 Place the foie gras on the burgers, top with the truffle slices, if using, and spoon the truffle glaze over. Serve with a mixed leaf salad and the ultimate fries alongside.

Trattoria burger on focaccia bianco, with white onion jam, and salsa verde drizzle

Here a well-flavored burger mix is thinly spread over the focaccia base, set on a bed of sweet onions, and topped with a lively, tangy salsa verde. Cut into small squares it makes a wonderful canapé to serve with drinks.

9 oz well-trimmed, coarsely ground beef
6 oz ground pork
1 onion, finely chopped
½ tsp ground cinnamon
1 tbsp fennel seeds, toasted
1 garlic clove, crushed
2 tbsp pine nuts, toasted
1 tbsp chopped fresh oregano
1 tbsp chopped fresh rosemary
2 tsp tomato purée
pinch of dried chili flakes
salt and freshly ground black pepper
1 ball of buffalo mozzarella, grated
¾ cup grated pecorino cheese
olive oil for cooking

Salsa verde
1 garlic clove, crushed
2 tbsp chopped fresh flat-leaf parsley
2 tbsp chopped fresh basil leaves
1 tbsp superfine capers, rinsed and dried
salt and freshly ground black pepper
1 anchovy fillet, rinsed, chopped
¼ tsp Dijon mustard
1 tsp balsamic vinegar
½ cup olive oil
• Place the garlic, herbs, capers, a little salt in a mortar and pestle, crush to a coarse paste; add the anchovy, mustard, vinegar, and crush again.
• Gradually add the oil to form a sauce, adjust the seasoning, and serve.

White onion jam
3 tbsp olive oil
1 tbsp unsalted butter
2 onions peeled, thinly sliced
3 tbsp sugar
1 tsp picked fresh thyme leaves
½ cup white wine vinegar
salt and freshly ground black pepper
• Heat the oil and butter in a pan, add the onions, sugar, and thyme; cook over a low heat for 10–12 minutes until golden, soft, and caramelized.
• Add the vinegar, cook for a further 10 minutes until the onions take on a sweet and sour flavor, remove, season to taste, and allow to go cold.

TO SERVE • 1 X RECIPE FOR FOCACCIA DOUGH (SEE PAGE 136)
• WHITE ONION JAM • SALSA VERDE

1 In a bowl, mix all the ingredients together except the mozzarella and percorino cheeses; season to taste, chill until needed.

2 Make the focaccia dough, following the recipe to the final stage, then roll it out to fit a shallow 8- x 10-inch baking tray, about ¼ inch thick.

3 Cover the base liberally with the white onion jam, then spread the meat evenly over the onions, and drizzle a little olive oil over.

4 Preheat the oven to 375°F.

5 Place the focaccia in the oven and bake for 15 minutes, then remove, sprinkle the grated cheeses over, and return to the oven for a further 10 minutes.

6 Remove and allow to cool before cutting into portions. Top each portion with a good drizzle of salsa verde before serving.

Tandoori lamb burger

Tandoori lamb burger with mint sambal and kachumbar piccalilli

1 lb 12 oz well-trimmed, coarsely ground
  lamb
1 onion, finely chopped
2 garlic cloves, crushed
2 tbsp plain yogurt
1 tbsp mango chutney
1-inch-piece ginger root, finely grated
1 tsp coriander seeds, crushed
1 tsp cumin seeds, crushed
½ tsp garam masala
¼ tsp turmeric
salt and freshly ground black pepper
pinch of cayenne
vegetable or sunflower oil for cooking

TO SERVE · 4 CUMIN NAAN BREADS,
WARMED · MINT SAMBAL · KACHUMBAR
PICCALILLI (SEE PAGE 128)

1 Place the lamb in a large bowl, add the onion, garlic, and yogurt; cover and leave for 30 minutes in the refrigerator.
2 Add all the remaining ingredients, mixing well, then return to the refrigerator. Leave overnight for the best results.
3 Divide the mix into 8 equal portions, then using wet hands roll each of them into a long sausage shape, brush them liberally with the oil.
4 Heat a chargrill or pan grill until hot, add the burgers, and cook for 5–6 minutes until cooked and lightly charred all over, turning them regularly.
5 Serve the burgers on the warm cumin naan breads, topped with the kachumbar piccalilli, and with the mint sambal alongside.

Mint sambal
⅓ cup Greek-style yogurt
2 onions, peeled, finely chopped
¼ tsp garam masala
1-inch-piece ginger root, finely
  grated
1 garlic clove, crushed
½ cup mint leaves
· Place all the ingredients in a blender and mix together; cover and chill for at least 2 hours, preferably overnight, before serving.

Souvlaki burger wraps with beet and horseradish tzatziki

1 lb 12 oz trimmed, coarsely ground lamb
½ cup crumbled feta cheese
1 onion, finely chopped
1 garlic clove, crushed
2 tbsp chopped fresh flat-leaf parsley
1 tbsp chopped fresh mint
2 tsp chopped fresh oregano
½ tsp ground cumin
salt and freshly ground black pepper
vegetable or sunflower oil for cooking
4 wooden skewers, soaked

1 Mix all the ingredients for the burgers together in a bowl, chill for 1 hour.
2 Using wet hands, mold the mix around 4 soaked and oiled wooden skewers in a sausage shape. Brush liberally with oil.
3 Heat a chargrill or pan grill until hot, add the skewers, and cook for 4–5 minutes until cooked and lightly charred, turning them regularly. Remove and keep them warm.
4 Place the flatbreads on the grill and char lightly, about 30–40 seconds on each side.
5 Sprinkle some iceberg lettuce, red onion and parsley over the base of each grilled flatbread. Spoon some beet and horseradish tzatziki over, then finally remove the skewers from the burgers and place on each flatbread.
6 Roll up the flatbreads to enclose, and eat immediately.

TO SERVE · 4 THIN MIDDLE EASTERN FLATBREADS · SHREDDED ICEBERG LETTUCE · 1 SMALL RED ONION, THINLY SLICED
· ½ CUP ROUGHLY CHOPPED FLAT-LEAF PARSLEY · BEET AND HORSERADISH TZATZIKI (SEE PAGE 128)

Souvlaki burger wraps

Sosatie burgers with peanut curry chiffonade, and apricot and red onion chutney

Traditionally sosaties are kabobs marinated in a thick, sweet curry sauce before being chargrilled over hot coals: a marrying of sweet and savory flavors originally introduced from Malaysia. These burgers are based on this theme.

1 lb 12 oz trimmed, coarsely ground lamb
1 onion, grated
1 garlic clove, crushed
2 tbsp apricot jam
1 tbsp curry powder
1 tsp ground coriander
¼ tsp ground ginger
¼ tsp turmeric
½ tsp grated lemon zest
salt and freshly ground black pepper
pinch of dried chili flakes
vegetable or sunflower oil for cooking
4 wooden skewers, soaked

1 Place the lamb in a large bowl, add all the remaining burger ingredients, and work together; do not overwork or the mix will toughen. Chill in the refrigerator for 1 hour.
2 Divide the mix into 12 small evenly sized balls then, with wet hands, roll into sausage shapes. Thread 3 sosaties on to each soaked skewer.
3 Heat a thin film of oil on a pan grill or in a frying pan and, when hot, add the burgers and cook for 4–5 minutes until cooked.
4 Run a knife along one side of the baby baguettes but do not cut right through. Open them, taking care not to split them.
5 Place the peanut curry chiffonade in the base of each baguette, top with sliced tomatoes then place a sosatie burger skewer on top and close the baguette.
6 Serve with the apricot and red onion chutney on the side. Some chunky fries also go well with this burger.

Peanut–curry chiffonade
3 tbsp good quality mayonnaise
1 tbsp smooth peanut butter
1 tsp balsamic vinegar
½ tsp soy sauce
½-inch-piece ginger root, finely grated
pinch of cumin
pinch of sugar
salt and freshly ground black pepper
¼ iceberg lettuce, cut into chiffonade (thin shreds)
· Mix all the ingredients except the lettuce together in a bowl, seasoning to taste; add the lettuce and bind together. Chill.

Apricot and red onion chutney
¾ cup thinly sliced dried apricots
1 Granny Smith apple, cored and chopped
⅓ cup soaked raisins
2 red onions, thinly sliced
⅓ cup brown sugar
½ cup red wine
2 tbsp corn or maple syrup
1 tbsp balsamic vinegar
· Place all the ingredients in a pan, add scant 1 cup of water and bring to a boil.
· Reduce the heat to a simmer, cover, and cook gently for 20–30 minutes.
· Uncover and continue to cook for a further 30 minutes until the onions are tender and no liquid remains. Allow to cool; store in an airtight jar ready for use.

TO SERVE · 4 BABY BAGUETTES · PEANUT–CURRY CHIFFONADE · 4 TOMATOES, THINLY SLICED · APRICOT AND RED ONION CHUTNEY

Lebanese kibbeh burger with smoked chili and white bean hummus

In the Middle Eastern countries making kibbeh is an art form that requires practice to achieve perfection. I love the smoked chili-style hummus that accompanies the dish—it really adds a great kick.

1 cup bulgur wheat
1 onion, finely grated
1 garlic clove, crushed
1 tsp ground allspice
½ tsp ground cumin
½ tsp ground coriander
¼ tsp sweet paprika
3 tbsp chopped fresh flat-leaf parsley
1 lb 6 oz well-trimmed, coarsely ground lamb
salt and freshly ground black pepper
vegetable or sunflower oil for cooking

1 Place the bulgur wheat in a bowl, pour over enough boiling water to cover; leave to soak for 30 minutes, then drain off any remaining water left in the bowl. Dry the bulgur wheat in a towel.

2 Place the bulgur wheat in a large bowl, add the onion, garlic, spices, and parsley, and allow to stand for 15 minutes.

3 Add the lamb and mix together, but do not overwork the mix. Adjust the seasoning.

4 Divide the mix into 8 evenly sized patties, then roll in the palm of your wet hands into classic torpedo oval shapes; brush with oil.

5 Heat a chargrill or pan grill until hot, add the burgers, and cook for 5–6 minutes or longer if preferred.

6 Open the pita breads without tearing them to form pockets; fill with the tomato, pomegranate, and parsley salad, tuck in the burgers, and serve with a dish of smoked chili and white bean hummus alongside.

Tomato, pomegranate, and parsley salad
1 tbsp sugar
1 tsp red wine vinegar
3 tbsp honey
1 garlic clove, crushed
½ cup sundried tomatoes in oil, drained, oil reserved
1 fresh pomegranate, halved
½ large bunch fresh flat-leaf parsley, picked and washed
3 tbsp pine nuts, toasted
salt and freshly ground black pepper
• In a pan heat the sugar and vinegar with the honey until dissolved.
• Add the garlic, tomatoes, and 3 tbsp of their oil, and cook for 1 minute. Remove to a bowl and allow to cool.
• Squeeze out the seeds from the pomegranate halves.
• Add the parsley, pomegranate seeds, and pine nuts, and season.

Smoked chili and white bean hummus
1 tbsp chipotle chilies
1 cup cooked cannellini beans (canned is fine)
2 tbsp tahini (sesame seed) paste
½ tsp ground cumin
3 tbsp olive oil
2 small garlic cloves, crushed
juice of ½ lemon
½ tsp salt
• Reconstitute the chipotle chilies in hot water for 30 minutes, drain and discard the water. Finely chop the chilies.
• Place the beans in a blender with the chilies and remaining ingredients, and mix to a smooth paste.
• According to taste add a little more garlic or lemon juice.
• Refrigerate overnight to infuse the flavors, covered with plastic wrap.

TO SERVE · 8 MINI PITA BREADS OR 4 PITA BREADS, HALVED · SMOKED CHILI AND WHITE BEAN HUMMUS · TOMATO, POMEGRANATE, AND PARSLEY SALAD

Lamb burger briks with smoked eggplant hash, and green harissa mayo

There is something mystical about Morocco—and its food is like its people: heartwarming. The flavors are delicate, yet simple. These Moroccan-style burgers are encased in a crisp pastry shell; the eggplant hash adds a warm smoky addition to the dish.

TO SERVE · FEW SALAD LEAVES TO GARNISH · GREEN HARISSA MAYO (SEE PAGE 126)

Smoked eggplant hash

1 eggplant
⅓ cup olive oil
1 small onion, finely chopped
1 garlic clove, crushed
1 anchovy fillet, rinsed, finely chopped
1 tsp smoked paprika or paprika
2 tbsp freshly chopped cilantro
salt and freshly ground black pepper

· Preheat oven to 400°F.
· Brush the eggplant all over with ⅓ of the olive oil.
· Place in the oven on a baking tray, bake for 30–35 minutes, turning it until it is soft and fairly charred in color. Remove and cool.
· Cut the eggplant in half lengthwise, scoop out the flesh and chop finely. Discard the skin.
· Heat the remaining oil in a frying pan, add the onion, garlic, anchovy, and paprika and cook for 4–5 minutes until soft.
· Add the chopped eggplant, mix well, and cook for 2–3 minutes, remove and cool. Add the chopped cilantro and season to taste.

1 onion, peeled, finely chopped

1 small green bell pepper, deseeded, finely chopped

2 tbsp chopped fresh cilantro

1-inch-piece ginger root, finely chopped

pinch of turmeric

1 lb 5 oz well-trimmed, coarsely ground lamb

1 tbsp green harissa mayo (see page 126)

salt and freshly ground black pepper

1 tbsp olive oil

8 sheets spring roll pastry

Smoked eggplant hash (see left)

1 egg, beaten with 1 tbsp milk

vegetable oil for deep frying

1 Place the onion, green bell pepper, cilantro, ginger, and turmeric in a food processor and mix to a coarse paste. Transfer to a large bowl, add the meat, harissa mayo, and season to taste. Bring the mixture together lightly, do not overwork it. Chill for 1 hour.

2 Divide the mix into 4 evenly sized burgers then, with your thumb, press down in the center of each burger to form an indentation.

3 Heat a film of olive oil in a large nonstick frying pan; when hot, add the burgers, cook for 2–3 minutes on each side, keeping them rare. Remove from the pan and cool.

4 Lay out 4 sheets of the spring roll pastry, place some smoked eggplant hash in the center and top with a burger.

5 Brush the outside edges with the beaten egg wash, fold the edges up and gently over the burger to enclose. Take the remaining 4 sheets and cover each burger to create a parcel, sealing the pastry neatly on top.

6 Half fill a deep-fat fryer or deep, heavy based saucepan with the oil and heat it to 350°F; carefully lower the briks into the oil and fry for 2–3 minutes until golden.

7 Remove to kitchen paper and drain well.

8 Garnish with salad leaves and serve with green harissa mayo.

Neo-classical feta burger with horiatiki salsa salad, and yogurt garlic sauce

Grilling the burgers in the vine leaves not only retains flavor and moistness, but also makes an unusual presentation. These little parcels can be made in advance then wrapped and kept in the refrigerator until needed.

24 brine-preserved vine leaves
1 lb 5 oz trimmed, coarsely ground lamb
1 garlic clove, crushed
1 tsp ground cumin
1 tsp ground coriander
1 egg yolk
salt and freshly ground black pepper
1 cup crumbled feta cheese
½ cup olive oil

Yogurt garlic sauce
½ cup Greek-style yogurt
2 garlic cloves, crushed
· Mix together in a bowl, season to taste.

1 Remove the vine leaves from the jar, rinse well under very cold water, then dry in a cloth.

2 Place the meat in a bowl, add the garlic, spices, and egg yolk. Season to taste.

3 Add the feta and just bring it together, but do not let it become overworked or packed too tightly.

4 Divide the mix into 8 evenly sized burgers.

5 Lay out 3 vine leaves on a flat surface, just overlapping each other.

6 Place a burger in the center of the leaves, then wrap it up carefully like a parcel and secure with 2 toothpicks; prepare the others in the same way. Brush the leaves liberally all over with the olive oil.

7 Heat a chargrill or pan grill until hot, add the vine-wrapped burgers and cook over a medium heat for 5–6 minutes, turning them regularly to ensure even cooking.

8 Serve with the horiatiki salsa salad and the yogurt garlic sauce on the side.

Horiatiki salsa salad

2 ripe but firm tomatoes, cut into chunks
1 small red onion, peeled, cut chunks
¼ cup peeled, diced cucumber
1 small green bell pepper, deseeded, diced
1 small green chili, deseeded, finely chopped
12 green olives
1 tbsp chopped fresh oregano
2 tbsp roughly chopped fresh mint leaves
¼ cup olive oil
Toss all the ingredients together in a bowl; leave
for 30 minutes to marinate prior to serving.

TO SERVE · HORIATIKI SALSA SALAD · YOGURT GARLIC SAUCE

Ginger–plum relish
⅔ cup pitted, chopped plums
  (canned are fine)
½ garlic clove, crushed
2 tbsp finely chopped stem ginger
1 tbsp Asian sweet chili sauce
• Mix all the ingredients in a bowl, cover with plastic wrap, and leave to infuse the flavors and marinate in the refrigerator for 24 hours.

Barbecue pork-belly burger

with sticky herb baste, ginger–plum relish, and pea and radish salad

The addition of some belly pork to the basic mix really adds a moistness and richness to the burger. The plum relish is a must! It may be kept refrigerated for up to a week.

1 lb well-trimmed, coarsely ground pork, chilled
10 oz coarsely ground rindless pork belly, chilled
2 tbsp chopped fresh cilantro
⅓ cup salted peanuts
1-inch-piece ginger root, finely grated
1 stick lemongrass, outer casing removed, very finely chopped
1 shallot, finely chopped
vegetable oil for cooking

FOR THE BASTE
¼ cup ketchup manis (Indonesian soy sauce) or light soy sauce
¼ cup dry sherry
2 tbsp chopped fresh cilantro
1 tbsp maple syrup
1 tsp ground aniseed
½ tsp dried chili flakes

8 wooden skewers, soaked

1 Place both ground meats in a bowl, add the remaining burger ingredients, and bring the mix together. Place all the ingredients for the baste in a bowl and mix well. Add 2 tbsp of the baste to the burger mix, mix well, taking care not to overwork. Place in the refrigerator, covered, for 1 hour.
2 Heat a chargrill or pan grill until very hot. Brush the grill with a little oil. Divide the burger mix into 4 evenly sized, oblong burgers and thread 2 wooden skewers through each of them.
3 Liberally brush the baste over the burgers and place on the grill, brushing them regularly with the baste, and turning them until cooked, about 4–5 minutes on each side. Their appearance should be glossy and they should be sticky in texture.
4 Arrange the pea salad on the plate and top with a burger. Garnish with fresh cilantro leaves and serve with a little ginger–plum relish.

TO SERVE · PEA AND RADISH SALAD · GINGER–PLUM RELISH · CILANTRO LEAVES TO GARNISH

Pea and radish salad
¾ cup sugar snap peas
½ cup snow peas
6 red radishes, thinly sliced
½ cup roughly chopped fresh mint leaves
1 tbsp light soy sauce
1 tbsp sugar
1 tbsp rice wine vinegar
1 tsp sesame oil
salt and freshly ground black pepper
• Blanch the peas separately in boiling water for 1 minute, then refresh in ice water. Drain, then dry well. Place in a bowl, add the radishes and chopped mint.
• Heat the soy, sugar and vinegar in a small pan for 1 minute, leave to cool. Add the sesame oil, pour over the salad, toss well together, season to taste and serve.

Bulgogi barbecue burgers baked in banana-leaf parcels

The flavors of the famous Korean barbecued beef dish are wonderful. Cooking in banana leaves keeps in all the aromas and natural juices. To make the leaves supple to wrap, hold them over a flame until they soften. If banana leaves are not available, use foil pouches.

1 lb 8 oz coarsely ground pork
3 scallions, finely chopped
1-inch-piece ginger root, finely grated
1 garlic clove, crushed
2 tbsp light soy sauce
1 tbsp Asian sweet chili sauce
2 tsp sesame oil
1 tsp sugar
½ tsp sesame seeds, toasted
vegetable or sunflower oil for cooking

1 Mix all the ingredients for the burgers in a bowl, chill for 1 hour.
2 Divide the mix into 4 evenly sized burgers and brush liberally with the oil.
3 Heat a film of oil in a nonstick frying pan and, when hot, add the burgers; brown on each side for 1 minute then remove.
4 Place a burger in the center of each banana leaf and spoon some of the mango–coconut cream sauce over. Carefully pull up the sides of the banana leaf to enclose the burgers and make a neat parcel. Secure tightly with toothpicks.
5 Heat a chargrill or pan grill until hot, add the parcels and cook for 12–15 minutes or, alternatively, place in a preheated oven for 8–10 minutes.
6 Remove the parcels from the grill and serve; let the guests open them to release the wonderful aromas.

TO SERVE · 4 SQUARES OF BANANA LEAF, ABOUT 10 X 10 INCHES · MANGO–COCONUT CREAM SAUCE (SEE PAGE 131)

Caribbean pork burgers with barbecue jerk baste and calypso mojo

1 lb well-trimmed, coarsely ground pork
3½ oz good quality sausage meat
1 onion, finely chopped
1 tbsp chopped fresh oregano
3 tbsp prepared jerk baste (see below)
salt and freshly ground black pepper
vegetable or sunflower oil for brushing

FOR THE JERK BASTE
3 tbsp olive oil
2 tbsp white wine vinegar
2 tbsp hot chili sauce
1 tbsp tomato ketchup
1 garlic clove, crushed
1 tsp dried thyme
1 tsp ground cinnamon
1 tsp sugar
1 tsp ground coriander
½ tsp ground allspice

1 For the baste, place all the ingredients in a blender and mix until smooth.
2 Place the meat and sausage meat in a bowl, add 3 tbsp water, the onion, oregano and 3 tbsp of the jerk baste. Adjust the seasoning, cover with plastic wrap and chill in the refrigerator for at least 1 hour.
3 Divide the mix into 8 evenly sized burgers and brush with oil.
4 Heat a chargrill or pan grill until hot, add the burgers and grill for 8–10 minutes until cooked through, brushing them during the process with more of the baste.
5 Toast the buns; top the bases with a slice of tomato, a few dressed leaves, then 2 burgers.
6 Spoon the calypso mojo over and top with cilantro leaves to garnish.

TO SERVE • 4 SESAME BURGER BUNS • 4 SLICES LARGE TOMATO • GREEN SALAD LEAVES DRESSED IN FRENCH DRESSING • CALYPSO MOJO (SEE PAGE 130) • FRESH CILANTRO LEAVES

Sicilian veal burger with bell peppers, olives, and pesto crostini

1 lb 12 oz coarsely ground veal
1 tbsp chopped fresh oregano
2 tbsp basil pesto
1 garlic clove, crushed
⅓ cup finely chopped black olives
1 red bell pepper, halved, deseeded, finely
  chopped
1 red onion, finely chopped
salt and freshly ground black pepper
vegetable or sunflower oil for cooking

1 Combine all the burger ingredients in a bowl, add 1 tablespoon of water, mix together well, and chill for 1 hour. Season the mix to taste and divide into 4 evenly sized burgers.
2 Heat a thin film of oil in a nonstick frying pan and, when hot, add the burgers and cook for 6–8 minutes until cooked.
3 Toast the ciabatta slices then spread with the basil pesto, top with tomato slices.
4 Top with the burger, then the shaved Parmesan cheese. Garnish with the dressed arugula leaves and serve. Serve the aioli sauce on the side.

TO SERVE • 4 SLICES CIABATTA BREAD • BASIL PESTO (SEE PAGE 126) • SLICED TOMATOES • ½ CUP FRESHLY SHAVED PARMESAN • ARUGULA LEAVES DRESSED IN BALSAMIC VINEGAR • AIOLI SAUCE (SEE PAGE 126)

Vitello tonnato burger with tuna and caper sauce

vegetable or sunflower oil for cooking
1 onion, finely chopped
1 tbsp chopped fresh rosemary
1 lb good quality, coarsely ground veal
  rump
10 oz ground pork
1 tsp Dijon mustard
salt and freshly ground black pepper

1 Heat 2 tbsp of the oil in a frying pan and, when hot, add the onion and rosemary, and cook for 4–5 minutes until softened. Transfer to a large bowl and allow to cool.
2 Add both meats, the mustard, salt and pepper to taste, and chill for 1 hour.
3 Divide the meat into 4 evenly sized burgers and brush liberally with oil.
4 Heat a thin film of oil in a large frying pan, add the burgers, and cook for 6–8 minutes or until cooked to your taste.
5 Split the focaccia in half horizontally to give 4 bases. Top each with some tuna and caper sauce, then top with a burger.
6 Top each burger with 2 slices of tomato and then with some arugula leaves, dressed in the black olive dressing. Sprinkle the toasted pine nuts over and serve.

Tuna and caper sauce
3½ oz canned tuna in oil, well
  drained
1 small garlic clove, crushed
2 anchovy fillets in oil, drained,
  chopped
2 tsp capers, rinsed, chopped
⅓ cup good quality mayonnaise
1 tbsp chopped fresh chives
1 tbsp fresh lemon juice
• Place the tuna, garlic, anchovies, and capers in a blender, mix to a smooth purée, remove to a bowl.
• Mix with the mayonnaise, chives, and lemon juice, seasoning to taste. Keep chilled ready for use.

Black olive dressing
⅓ cup pitted and finely chopped
  black olives
⅓ cup olive oil
juice of ½ lemon
1 tsp balsamic vinegar
2 tbsp chopped fresh chives
• Mix all the ingredients together, seasoning to taste.

TO SERVE • 2 X 4-INCH SQUARES FOCACCIA BREAD • TUNA AND CAPER SAUCE • 8 SLICES LARGE TOMATOES • ½ CUP ARUGULA LEAVES, WASHED • ¼ CUP BLACK OLIVE DRESSING • 2 TBSP TOASTED PINE NUTS

Cordon bleu burger with melting Brie and caramelized apple butter

1 lb 8 oz well-trimmed, coarsely ground
  chicken
1 onion, finely chopped
1 tbsp chopped fresh rosemary
salt and freshly ground black pepper
vegetable or sunflower oil for cooking
4 oz thinly sliced gammon ham
5 tsp superfine sugar
1 Granny Smith apple, peeled, cored, cut
  into small chunks
2 tbsp unsalted butter
4 x ½-inch-thick wedges of Brie cheese

1 Combine the chicken with scant ¼ cup water, the onion, and rosemary in a bowl, season to taste; cover and refrigerate for 1 hour.
2 Divide into 4 evenly sized burgers and brush liberally with oil.
3 Heat a chargrill or pan grill until very hot, add the burgers, and cook for 4–5 minutes each side or longer if you prefer; keep them warm. Grill the ham slices on each side, keep warm.
4 Meanwhile heat the sugar in a pan, add the apple pieces and cook until lightly caramelized; add the butter and 2 tbsp water, cover with a lid, and cook to a compote; season to taste.
5 Place a wedge of Brie cheese on each burger and place under a preheated broiler until the cheese is just melted.
6 Place some watercress in the base of each roll, followed by a slice of gammon ham. Top with a burger and a good spoonful of caramelized apple butter, cover with the roll lid and serve immediately.

TO SERVE · 4 CRUSTY ROLLS, SPLIT · ½ CUP WATERCRESS LEAVES

Chicken steak burger with Provençal flavors

1 lb 7 oz skinless, boneless chicken breast
salt and freshly ground black pepper
2 cups panko crumbs or fresh white bread
    crumbs
⅓ cup milk
2 tbsp chopped fresh basil
½ cup finely grated Parmigiano Reggianno
    cheese
flour for dusting
2 eggs, beaten
vegetable oil or sunflower oil for cooking
4 slices firm goat cheese log

1 Place the chicken and a little seasoning in a food processor with ⅓ of the panko crumbs and mix to a coarse pulp. Add the milk, mix again for 20 seconds. Add the chopped basil then remove to a bowl and chill for 30 minutes.
2 Flour your hands and shape the mix into 4 evenly sized burgers.
3 Mix the remaining panko crumbs and Parmesan. Pass the burgers through extra flour, then through the beaten egg wash, then into the panko Parmesan mix; reshape if necessary.
4 Heat a thin film of oil in a nonstick frying pan, add the burgers and fry until golden.
5 Toast the buns and spoon some mayonnaise on the bases, add a few arugula leaves and some basil pesto.
6 Place the chicken burger on top, then a slice of the goat cheese. Place under a hot grill for 30 seconds to melt the cheese. Drizzle some black olive tapenade over, close the buns, and serve.

Black olive tapenade
1 anchovy fillet, rinsed, chopped
2 tbsp superfine capers
3 tbsp pitted black olives
⅓ cup olive oil
1 garlic cove, crushed
2 tbsp chopped fresh flat-leaf parsley
salt and freshly ground black pepper
• Place all the ingredients in a blender and mix to a coarse paste; adjust seasoning and serve.

TO SERVE • 4 PLAIN BUNS, SPLIT • ¼ CUP MAYONNAISE (SEE PAGE 126) • ARUGULA SALAD DRESSED IN BALSAMIC DRESSING • BASIL PESTO • (SEE PAGE 126) • BLACK OLIVE TAPENADE

Smoked chicken cobb burger with watercress and tomato yogurt

The idea for this burger came from the classical American cobb salad that I just enjoyed in Florida. I loved the idea of chicken, avocado, and blue cheese in harmony and I decided to create a smoked chicken burger around the theme.

1 lb well-trimmed, coarsely ground chicken breast
9 oz skinless smoked chicken breasts, finely diced
1 small onion, finely chopped
1 tsp Dijon mustard
1 tbsp tomato ketchup
1 tsp hot chili sauce
1 tbsp sour cream
salt and freshly ground black pepper
vegetable or sunflower oil for cooking

1 In a bowl mix together the chicken breast with the finely diced smoked chicken.
2 Add the onion, mustard, ketchup, and chili sauce, and bind together; add the sour cream and seasoning and bind together for a final time. Chill for 1 hour in the refrigerator.
3 Using wet hands, divide the mix into 4 evenly sized burgers. Brush the burgers liberally with the oil.
4 Heat a chargrill or pan grill until hot, add the burgers, and cook for 4–5 minutes on each side until golden.
5 Toast the muffins or buns on the grill pan until golden, top with some shredded endive. Add the burger and then some sliced avocado and thinly sliced onion.
6 Finally sprinkle the crumbled blue cheese over and pass under a hot broiler to melt the cheese; serve with the watercress and tomato yogurt.

Watercress and tomato yogurt
½ cup watercress, stalks removed
2 plum tomatoes, peeled, deseeded, chopped
1 small red onion, finely chopped
scant ½ cup sour cream
3 tbsp canned corn kernels, drained
salt and freshly ground black pepper
• Mix all the ingredients together in a bowl, season to taste.

Barbecue chicken burger

with Thai spices, green chili relish, and coconut–lemongrass chutney

The ingredients in this Asian burger are typical of Thai cooking, giving it a sensual flavor and aroma, and they are all now easily accessible for the cook. When preparing the chili relish use a mild variety.

1 tbsp red curry paste (rempah)
2 sticks lemongrass, tough outer casing removed, very finely chopped
¼ tsp turmeric
1-inch-piece ginger root, peeled, finely grated
1 lb ground chicken breast, well chilled
9 oz ground pork, well chilled

3 kaffir lime leaves, finely chopped
2 tbsp chopped fresh Thai basil (holy basil)
1 tbsp chopped fresh cilantro
2 tbsp coconut milk
pinch each ground cumin and ground coriander
salt and freshly ground black pepper
vegetable oil for cooking

1 In a bowl mix together the curry paste, lemongrass, turmeric, and ginger. Add the ground meats and mix well with wet hands to bring all the ingredients together.
2 Add the lime leaves, fresh herbs, coconut milk, ground spices, and seasoning. Bring together again, but do not overwork. Place in the refrigerator to chill.
3 With wet hands, shape into 4 evenly sized burgers. Heat a pan grill.
4 Brush the burgers with a little oil, place on the grill, and cook for 6–8 minutes until golden and cooked, turning them regularly.
5 Toast the burger buns, spread the bottom buns liberally with the green chili relish, and top each with a slice of large tomato.
6 Place the burgers on top and garnish with the coconut–lemongrass chutney; close with the lid and serve.

Green chili relish

scant ½ cup rice wine vinegar
⅓ cup soft brown sugar
½ cup raisins, soaked in water for 15 minutes, then drained
2 shallots, finely chopped
2 green bell peppers, deseeded, chopped
5 oz mild green chilies, deseeded, finely chopped (Dutch lombok variety)
½ tbsp chopped ginger root
1 garlic clove, crushed
1 tsp nam pla (fish sauce)
• Place the vinegar and sugar in a small pan and bring to a boil. Add the raisins and cook to a light caramel, the liquid should be syrupy.
• Stir in the shallots, green bell pepper, chilies, ginger, and garlic. Cook for 3-4 minutes, add the fish sauce, then remove from the heat and leave to cool.
• Place in a blender, mix to a coarse purée, serve chilled.

Coconut–lemongrass chutney

9 oz red cherry tomatoes
3 tbsp honey
juice of 3 limes
1 fresh coconut, outer shell removed, coarsely grated
2 tbsp unsalted peanuts
1 small green chili, deseeded, finely chopped
1 tbsp chopped pickled pink ginger
2 sticks lemongrass, outer casing removed, finely chopped
2 tbsp coarsely chopped fresh cilantro
1 tbsp coarsely chopped fresh mint
• Cut the cherry tomatoes in half, and place in a bowl, add the honey and lime juice, leave for 30 minutes to release their juices.
• Add the remaining ingredients, toss well together, leave to marinate for a further 2 hours before use.

TO SERVE · 4 BURGER BUNS, SPLIT · 4 SLICES LARGE TOMATO · GREEN CHILI RELISH · COCONUT–LEMONGRASS CHUTNEY

Bengali chicken burger with cucumber and tomato achar, and Asian guacamole

Bengal lies in the northeast of India; it is famed for its art and wonderful food festivals which are an everyday part of Bengali life. The popular blend of spices used in this burger is more commonly known as 'panch phoran': a five-spice mixture with a unique flavor.

¼ tsp fennel seeds

¼ tsp cumin seeds

¼ tsp black cumin (kalongi)

⅛ tsp black mustard seeds

⅛ tsp fenugreek

1 lb 7 oz coarsely ground, skinless, boneless chicken breast

5 oz good quality sausage meat

salt and freshly ground black pepper

vegetable or sunflower oil for cooking

1 Heat a dry, nonstick frying pan and, when hot, add the fennel seeds, cumin, black cumin, mustard seeds, and fenugreek, and toss for 30 seconds so that they give off their aroma and fragrance.

2 Place in a mortar and pestle and crush to a fine powder.

3 Place both meats in a bowl, add the crushed spices, and season to taste. Chill for 1 hour.

4 Divide the mix into 4 evenly sized burgers and brush liberally with oil.

5 Heat a chargrill or pan grill until hot, add the burgers and cook for 6–8 minutes until golden.

6 Toast the buns; place some Asian guacamole on the base of each and top each with a cooked burger. Spoon the cucumber and tomato achar over, close the lid, and serve. Serve the sour cream alongside.

TO SERVE • 4 SESAME SEED BURGER BUNS, SPLIT (SEE PAGE 135) • ASIAN GUACAMOLE (SEE PAGE 130) • CUCUMBER AND TOMATO ACHAR • ¼ CUP SOUR CREAM

Cucumber and tomato achar

1 tbsp vegetable oil

1 onion, chopped

1 garlic clove, crushed

1 tsp curry paste

4 tomatoes, skinned, deseeded, diced

¼ cucumber, peeled, cut into ¼-inch dice

salt

lime juice to taste

2 tbsp chopped fresh cilantro

• Heat the oil in a small pan, add the onion and garlic, and cook for 3–4 minutes until tender. Add the curry paste and cook for a further 2 minutes.

• Add the tomatoes and cucumber; cook for 2–3 minutes until they begin to soften. Season to taste.

• Remove to a bowl, allow to go cold. Add the lime juice to give it a sour note, stir in the cilantro, and serve.

Chermoula burgers with minted harissa salsa, and preserved lemon and artichoke salad

Chermoula is a fragrant, aromatic Moroccan spice paste, used as a sauce or as a marinade base for flavoring fish, meats, and vegetables. In this recipe the ground spices permeate the meats lending an exotic flavor to a simple preparation.

1 lb 7oz coarsely ground skinless, boneless chicken breast

4 oz merguez or chorizo sausage, cut into ¼-inch dice

1 onion, peeled, finely chopped

1 garlic clove, crushed

1 small green chili, deseeded, finely chopped

1 tsp cumin seeds, toasted, crushed

1 tbsp coriander seeds, toasted, crushed

¼ tsp paprika

¼ tsp turmeric

salt and freshly ground black pepper

vegetable or sunflower oil for cooking

4 wooden skewers, soaked

1 Mix all the ingredients for the burgers in a bowl with 2 tbsp of water. Season the mixture to taste and chill for 1 hour.

2 Divide the mix into 8 evenly sized burgers, then, with wet hands, shape each burger around a wooden skewer in a sausage shape; brush liberally with oil.

3 Heat a chargrill or pan grill until hot, place the skewers on it, and chargrill for 6–8 minutes, turning them regularly and keeping the exposed part of the wooden skewer away from the heat to avoid burning.

4 Open the flatbreads, remove the burgers from the skewers, and place inside, then spoon some harissa salsa over. Serve with the preserved lemon and artichoke salad.

TO SERVE · 4 WARM MIDDLE EASTERN FLATBREADS OR PITAS · MINTED HARISSA SALSA · PRESERVED LEMON AND ARTICHOKE SALAD

Preserved lemon and artichoke salad

5 oz preserved artichokes in oil, drained (oil reserved), cut in half
1 garlic clove, crushed
2 tbsp flaked almonds, toasted
1 tbsp preserved lemon, finely diced
¼ cup honey
juice of 1 lemon
2 tbsp chopped fresh cilantro

• Heat 2 tbsp of the artichoke oil in a pan, add the garlic, and cook for 20 seconds. Add the almonds, preserved lemon, and honey, and cook for 2 minutes longer. Add the lemon juice, mix well.
• Pour into a bowl, add the artichokes, mix well to meld the flavors and leave to go cold.
• Sprinkle the cilantro over and serve.

Minted harissa salsa

4 plum tomatoes, skinned, deseeded, chopped
2 scallions, chopped
1 red onion, chopped
2 tbsp chopped fresh mint
1 tbsp maple syrup
½ garlic cove, crushed
juice of ½ lemon
½ tsp good quality harissa sauce

• Mix all the ingredients together; for the best flavor, leave to infuse overnight in the refrigerator.

Bacon-wrapped turkey burger

with melted Camembert, and spicy cranberry–green peppercorn relish

1 lb 12 oz coarsely ground skinless turkey breast, chilled

1 tsp Dijon mustard

2 tbsp chopped fresh flat-leaf parsley

1 tbsp unsalted butter

2 scallions, finely chopped

2 tsp picked fresh thyme leaves

1 small garlic clove, crushed

salt and freshly ground black pepper

vegetable or sunflower oil for cooking

8 slices bacon

olive oil

¼ Camembert cheese

1 In a bowl mix together the ground turkey, 1 tbsp of water, the mustard, and parsley.

2 Heat the butter in a small frying pan and, when hot, add the scallions, half the thyme, the garlic, and cook for 1 minute. Allow to cool, then add to the turkey mixture; season to taste. Chill in the refrigerator for up to 1 hour.

3 Form the mix into 4 evenly sized burgers. Wrap each burger in 2 slices of bacon, then secure each with a toothpick. Brush the burgers with a little olive oil.

4 Heat a chargrill or pan grill until very hot. Place the burgers on the grill and cook for 5 minutes on each side or until cooked through.

5 Using a cookie cutter, cut out a 3–3½-inch circle out of each slice of brioche and toast under a preheated broiler. Place some watercress on each of the brioche slices, then top with the burger.

6 Cut the Camembert into ½-inch-thick slices and place one on each burger. Sprinkle the remaining thyme over, drizzle with a little olive oil, and place under the broiler again until the cheese begins to melt. Top with a dollop of the relish, garnish with a thyme sprig, and serve.

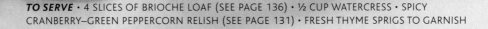

TO SERVE · 4 SLICES OF BRIOCHE LOAF (SEE PAGE 136) · ½ CUP WATERCRESS · SPICY CRANBERRY–GREEN PEPPERCORN RELISH (SEE PAGE 131) · FRESH THYME SPRIGS TO GARNISH

Turkey BLT burger stack

1 lb 5 oz ground skinless turkey
   breast
1 tsp Dijon mustard
1 tsp chopped fresh oregano
1 tsp Worcestershire sauce
1 tsp tomato ketchup
salt and freshly ground black
   pepper
vegetable or sunflower oil for
   cooking
4 long wooden skewers

FOR THE LETTUCE MAYONNAISE
¼ cup good quality mayonnaise
½ cup shredded iceberg lettuce
1 small onion, finely chopped
½ tsp American-style mustard
⅓ cup finely chopped dill pickles

1 Mix all the hamburger ingredients in a bowl
   with 1 tbsp water, chill for 1 hour.
2 Divide the mix into 8 evenly sized burgers,
   brush liberally with the oil.
3 Heat a chargrill or pan grill until very hot.
   Place the burgers on the grill and cook for
   4–5 minutes or longer if preferred. Grill the
   smoked bacon.
4 Mix all the ingredients together for the
   lettuce mayonnaise, season to taste.
5 Cut the buns into 3 horizontal slices and
   toast the bun slices. Place a good
   spoonful of cooked tomato relish on
   the base buns.
6 Top each with a burger, then some
   lettuce mayonnaise, and grilled
   bacon. Add a toasted slice of
   bun and another spoonful of
   tomato relish.
7 Finally add some tomato
   slices, grilled bacon, a second
   burger, and more lettuce
   mayonnaise. Close with the bun
   lid and plunge a wooden skewer
   into the center to keep it in place.

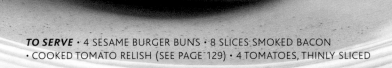

TO SERVE · 4 SESAME BURGER BUNS · 8 SLICES SMOKED BACON
· COOKED TOMATO RELISH (SEE PAGE 129) · 4 TOMATOES, THINLY SLICED

Peking duck wraps with hoisin barbecue sauce

These delicate, little pastry-wrapped triangles are filled with a Chinese-style patty; cooked Peking duck can be found in most supermarkets now. These wraps can be frozen then cooked when needed, although they will take an extra 10 minutes to cook.

10 oz skinless, boneless chicken breast

12 oz cooked Peking duck, meat and skin only

2 tbsp vegetable oil

2 tbsp oyster sauce

2 tbsp chopped fresh cilantro

1 small garlic clove, crushed

1 tsp Chinese five-spice mixture

1 tsp barbecue hoisin sauce

½ small red chili, deseeded, finely chopped

salt and freshly ground black pepper

8 sheets phyllo pastry (7 x 12 inches)

¼ cup butter, melted, for brushing

Hoisin barbecue sauce

1 tbsp dark brown sugar
2 tbsp tomato ketchup
1 garlic clove, crushed
1-inch piece ginger root
1 tsp rice wine vinegar
⅓ cup hoisin sauce
2 tbsp Asian sweet chili sauce
1 star anis pod
½ tbsp finely chopped
   lemongrass
• In a pan, combine the sugar, ketchup, garlic, and ginger with the vinegar; bring to a boil. Add the hoisin, sweet chili sauce, the star anise, lemongrass and ⅔ cup water. Simmer for 15–20 minutes, until reduced by one-third in volume. Remove the star anise and transfer the sauce to a bowl; allow to go cold before serving.

TO SERVE • FRESH CILANTRO LEAVES TO GARNISH • HOISIN BARBECUE SAUCE

1 Preheat oven to 400°F. Place the chicken meat and cooked duck in a food processor and mix to a coarse paste. Add the remaining filling ingredients and mix again quickly until incorporated; season to taste. Using wet hands, shape the mix into 8 evenly sized balls.
2 Fold one sheet of phyllo in half lengthwise, then fold over the corner at one end of the the pastry strip, over one meatball, covering it in a triangle shape. (Wonton wraps or spring roll pastry can also be used.)
3 Continue folding over the triangle of pastry along the length of the phyllo pastry strip to make a neat triangular samosa shape. Make 3 more samosa shapes in the same way.
4 Place them on a baking sheet, brush liberally with melted butter all over, and bake for 12–15 minutes or until golden. Garnish with fresh cilantro leaves and serve with the hoisin barbecue sauce separately.

Pheasant burger with foie gras, honey mustard glaze, and spicy kumquat chutney

Every year I eagerly look forward to the game season—and a real gourmet treat. The addition of a little pork and foie gras to these burgers adds flavor and also keeps them moist and juicy. The spicy cranberry–green peppercorn relish on page 131 would go well.

14 oz coarsely ground skinless, boneless
   pheasant breast
10 oz coarsely ground pork
3½ oz fresh foie gras, deveined, cut into
   ¼-inch cubes
1 shallot, finely chopped
4 juniper berries, finely chopped
2 tsp chopped fresh sage
salt and freshly ground black pepper
vegetable or sunflower oil for cooking

FOR THE GLAZE
1 tsp Dijon mustard
⅓ cup honey
1 tbsp olive oil
½ tsp soy sauce

1 In a bowl combine the pheasant, pork, and foie gras. Add the shallot, juniper, and sage along with a little salt and pepper, chill for 1 hour.
2 Divide the mix into 4 evenly sized burgers.
3 Heat a chargrill or pan grill until very hot, and brush the burgers liberally with oil.
4 Combine the ingredients for the glaze in a bowl.
5 Place the burgers on the grill and cook for 5–8 minutes, brushing them regularly with the glaze as they cook.
6 Toast the buns, and top the 4 bases with some spicy kumquat chutney, then with some arugula leaves, followed by the glazed pheasant burger, and serve.

Spicy kumquat chutney
1 cup sugar
1½ cups white wine vinegar
1 lb kumquats, halved
1 jalepeño chili, deseeded, finely
  chopped
1-inch piece ginger root, finely
  grated
• Place the sugar and vinegar in a pan and bring to a boil, stirring, to dissolve the sugar. When boiled, raise the heat and add the kumquats, chili, and ginger. Simmer gently for 30 minutes until the mix becomes thick and jam-like in consistency.
• Cool before use, serve warm or cold.

TO SERVE • 2 CHORIZO BURGER BUNS, SPLIT (SEE PAGE 135) • SPICY KUMQUAT CHUTNEY • ½ CUP ARUGULA LEAVES

Ostrich burger with cumin seed and guava ketchup, and tempura sweet potatoes

1 tsp cumin seeds
1 lb cleaned ostrich fillet, coarsely ground
9 oz ground pork
1 tbsp olive oil
1 garlic clove, crushed
½ tsp freshly grated orange zest
½ tsp ground cinnamon
salt and freshly ground black pepper
vegetable or sunflower oil for cooking

1 Heat a dry frying pan over a medium heat, add the cumin seeds, and dry fry for 10–15 seconds, keeping them moving so they do not burn. Transfer to a mortar and pestle and crush to a fine powder.

2 Place both meats in a bowl with 3 tbsp water; add the cumin seeds, olive oil, garlic, orange zest, and cinnamon. Mix well together but do not overwork; season to taste. Chill for 1 hour.

3 Divide the mix into 4 evenly sized burgers and brush liberally with oil.

4 Heat a chargrill or pan grill until very hot, add the burgers, and cook for 4–5 minutes on each side until cooked.

5 Toast the burger buns, spread a thin layer of mustard on the bases. Place some shredded iceberg lettuce on each base.

6 Top each base with a burger, then pour over a little cumin seed and guava ketchup, and top with a lid. Serve with tempura sweet potatoes on the side.

Cumin seed and guava ketchup
½ cup guava jam
2 tbsp tomato ketchup
1 tbsp treacle or molasses
2 tbsp red wine vinegar
1 tsp Dijon mustard
1 tsp ground cumin seeds
1 garlic clove
¼ tsp ground cinnamon
pinch of ground cloves
• Combine all the ingredients in a pan. Bring to a boil, reduce the heat, and cook for 15 minutes. Remove from the heat; allow to go cold before use.

TO SERVE • 4 BURGER BUNS, SPLIT • DIJON MUSTARD • SHREDDED ICEBERG LETTUCE
• CUMIN SEED AND GUAVA KETCHUP • TEMPURA SWEET POTATOES (SEE PAGE 140)

Green papaya ponzu sauce

juice of 1 lime
¼ cup olive oil
1 tsp rice wine vinegar
1 green papaya, peeled, finely sliced
½ small red chili, deseeded, finely shredded
3 scallions, finely shredded lengthwise
1 roasted red bell pepper, deseeded, finely shredded
2 tbsp chopped fresh cilantro
• Combine the lime juice, olive oil, and vinegar in a bowl. Add the fruit and vegetables, toss gently together. Add the cilantro and leave for 30 minutes to infuse the flavors.

TO SERVE
• 4 SESAME BURGER BUNS, SPLIT
• ⅓ CUP THINLY SLICED CUCUMBER
• WASABI MAYO (SEE PAGE 126)
• GREEN PAPAYA PONZU SAUCE
• CILANTRO LEAVES TO GARNISH
• SHISO CRESS TO GARNISH

5-spice rubbed quail burger with green papaya ponzu sauce, and wasabi mayo

1 lb 5 oz well-trimmed, coarsely ground, skinless, boneless quail
7oz ground turkey breast
4 scallions, finely chopped
1 red chili, deseeded, finely chopped
1 garlic clove, crushed
1-inch piece ginger root, finely grated
1 tbsp light soy sauce
1 tsp Chinese five-spice mixture
salt and freshly ground black pepper
vegetable or sunflower oil for cooking

1 Place the quail and turkey breast meat in a bowl with 3 tbsp water, add the scallions, red chili, garlic clove, ginger, soy sauce, half the five-spice mixture, and salt and pepper, and mix well. Cover with plastic wrap and chill for 1 hour.
2 Divide the mix into 4 evenly sized burgers, brush liberally with oil all over, then season with the remaining five-spice mixture.
3 Heat a chargrill or pan grill until hot, add the burgers, and cook for 4–5 minutes until cooked, or a little longer if you prefer.
4 Toast the buns; cover the bases with sliced cucumber.
5 Top with a good dollop of wasabi mayo, followed by the burgers.
6 Top with the green papaya ponzu sauce, cilantro leaves, and shiso cress. Replace the lids and serve.

Venison burger with grilled pineapple, and chili mayo

Andrew Blake is a talented restaurateur from Australia, and this recipe is from his magnificent book published some years ago called *Blakes*—and demonstrates a wonderful yet simple combination of ingredients.

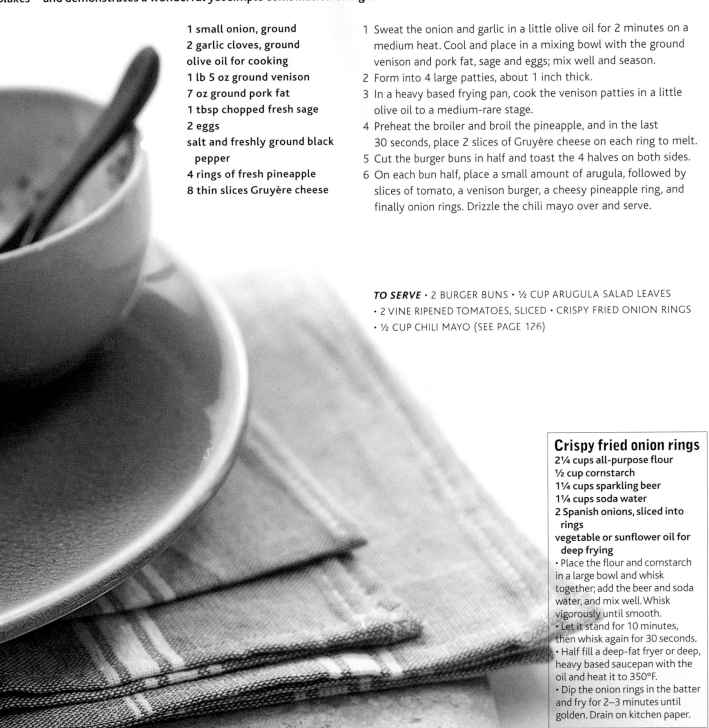

1 small onion, ground
2 garlic cloves, ground
olive oil for cooking
1 lb 5 oz ground venison
7 oz ground pork fat
1 tbsp chopped fresh sage
2 eggs
salt and freshly ground black
  pepper
4 rings of fresh pineapple
8 thin slices Gruyère cheese

1 Sweat the onion and garlic in a little olive oil for 2 minutes on a medium heat. Cool and place in a mixing bowl with the ground venison and pork fat, sage and eggs; mix well and season.
2 Form into 4 large patties, about 1 inch thick.
3 In a heavy based frying pan, cook the venison patties in a little olive oil to a medium-rare stage.
4 Preheat the broiler and broil the pineapple, and in the last 30 seconds, place 2 slices of Gruyère cheese on each ring to melt.
5 Cut the burger buns in half and toast the 4 halves on both sides.
6 On each bun half, place a small amount of arugula, followed by slices of tomato, a venison burger, a cheesy pineapple ring, and finally onion rings. Drizzle the chili mayo over and serve.

TO SERVE • 2 BURGER BUNS • ½ CUP ARUGULA SALAD LEAVES • 2 VINE RIPENED TOMATOES, SLICED • CRISPY FRIED ONION RINGS • ½ CUP CHILI MAYO (SEE PAGE 126)

Crispy fried onion rings
2¼ cups all-purpose flour
½ cup cornstarch
1¼ cups sparkling beer
1¼ cups soda water
2 Spanish onions, sliced into
  rings
vegetable or sunflower oil for
  deep frying
• Place the flour and cornstarch in a large bowl and whisk together; add the beer and soda water, and mix well. Whisk vigorously until smooth.
• Let it stand for 10 minutes, then whisk again for 30 seconds.
• Half fill a deep-fat fryer or deep, heavy based saucepan with the oil and heat it to 350°F.
• Dip the onion rings in the batter and fry for 2–3 minutes until golden. Drain on kitchen paper.

Pesto salmon burger

Pesto salmon burger with balsamic grilled asparagus

1 lb 5 oz fresh skinless, boneless salmon
  fillet, cut into large chunks
2 tbsp basil pesto (homemade or bought)
1 egg white
1 cup fresh white bread crumbs
1 shallot, peeled, finely chopped
salt and freshly ground black pepper
olive oil for cooking

Balsamic grilled asparagus
12 asparagus spears, peeled,
  woody base stem removed
2 tbsp olive oil
2 tsp balsamic vinegar
¼ tsp Dijon mustard
• Blanch the asparagus spears in boiling
salted water for 2 minutes, then remove with
a slotted spoon. Dry on a kitchen towel.
• Heat a chargrill or pan grill until hot. In a
bowl combine the oil, vinegar, and mustard
to form a paste.
• Pass the asparagus spears through the
mixture and place on the hot grill to cook
until golden and lightly charred, basting
regularly, about 3–4 minutes in total.

1 Place the salmon, basil pesto, egg white, bread crumbs, shallot, and salt and pepper in a food processor and mix until the salmon is finely chopped, but not puréed. Chill in the refrigerator for 30 minutes.
2 Divide the mixture into 8 evenly sized salmon burgers.
3 Heat a little olive oil in a large nonstick frying pan over medium heat. Add the burgers and cook for 2–3 minutes on each side until golden; do not overcook.
4 Cut the focaccia in half horizontally and toast them, then brush the cut sides with the oil.
5 To serve, arrange 3 asparagus on each toasted focaccia. Top each with 2 salmon burgers.
6 Place a good dollop of marscapone on top, followed by a drizzle of basil pesto, and garnish with the basil leaves.

TO SERVE · 2 X 4-INCH SQUARES FOCACCIA BREAD · BALSAMIC GRILLED ASPARAGUS
· 6 TBSP MARSCAPONE CHEESE · ¼ CUP BASIL PESTO (SEE PAGE 126)
· FRESH BASIL LEAVES TO GARNISH

Fajita salmon burger

1 lb fresh skinless, boneless salmon fillet,
  well chilled
salt and freshly ground black pepper
½ tsp paprika
1 egg white
2 cups fresh white bread crumbs
vegetable or sunflower oil for cooking
1 onion, thinly sliced
1 garlic clove, crushed
½ tsp chopped fresh oregano
1 small red bell pepper, roasted, shredded
pinch of chili powder
1 cup grated Monterey Jack or cheddar
  cheese

1 Place the salmon fillet in a food processor with a little salt, paprika, and the egg white, and mix to a smooth purée. Add the bread crumbs, mix again, season to tase, and remove to a bowl. Chill for 1 hour.
2 Divide the mix into 4 evenly sized balls, then roll out using wet hands to sausage shapes about 1 inch thick.
3 Heat a thin film of oil in a frying pan and, when hot, add the burgers and cook for 4–5 minutes until cooked; keep the burgers warm.
4 Return the pan to the heat, add a little more oil, the onion and garlic, and cook for 2–3 minutes. Add the oregano, shredded red bell pepper, chili powder, and cook for 1 minute. Stir in the cheese and immediately remove from the heat.
5 Using a dry frying pan, heat it until hot, add the tortillas one at a time and lightly char on each side; keep them warm.
6 Place one cooked burger in each tortilla, spoon the red bell pepper mix over, and roll up to secure. Cut each in half on a diagonal. Arrange 2 halves on each serving plate, spoon the tomato salsa over, and top with a good dollop of sour cream; garnish with lime wedges and cilantro leaves.

TO SERVE · 4 FLOUR TORTILLAS · FRESH TOMATO SALSA (SEE PAGE 131) · ½ CUP SOUR CREAM · LIME WEDGES · FRESH CILANTRO LEAVES TO GARNISH

Fajita salmon burger

Miso-basted salmon burger with hot mango–cucumber salsa, and cool chili verde

Miso is a Japanese condiment made from bean paste that embodies the essence of Japanese cooking. There are different types of miso—in this recipe the rich flavor of salmon is delicately combined with a sweet and savory glaze made using white miso.

1 lb 5 oz fresh skinless, boneless salmon fillet
1 tsp white miso paste
2 tbsp vegetable oil
1 shallot, finely chopped
1-inch-piece ginger root, peeled, finely chopped
salt
1½ cups fresh white bread crumbs
2 scallions, finely chopped
1 large egg white
1 tbsp light soy sauce
1 tsp sesame oil
½ tsp mustard seeds

FOR THE GLAZE
½ tbsp white miso paste
2 tbsp maple syrup
1 tsp soy sauce

1 In a small bowl, mix together the ingredients for the glaze and set aside.
2 Place 12 oz of the salmon in a food processor with 1 tsp of the miso and mix to a fine paste. Finely chop the remaining salmon. Chill separately in the refrigerator for 20 minutes.
3 Heat 1 tbsp of the vegetable oil in a small pan, add the shallot and ginger, and cook until softened but with no color; remove and allow to cool.
4 Remove the processed and chopped salmon from the refrigerator, place in a bowl; add the cooked shallot and ginger, a little salt, and mix well.
5 Add the remaining ingredients and bring the mix together, shape into 4 evenly sized burgers, and return to the refrigerator until needed.
6 Heat the remaining oil in a large nonstick frying pan until hot, cook the salmon burgers until golden, about 3–4 minutes on each side, brushing them regularly with the glaze as they cook.
7 Arrange the lettuce leaves on the 4 crusty rolls, top each with a burger, and then with some mango–cucumber salsa. Top with the remaining bread. Serve with a little pot of cool chili verde on the side.

Hot mango–cucumber salsa
1 small mango, stone removed, cut in thin slices
¼ cucumber, cut in ribbons lengthwise, using a vegetable peeler
1 tsp sugar
2 tbsp lime juice
salt
good pinch of dried chili flakes
• Place all the ingredients together in a bowl, toss well together, leave until required.

Cool chili verde
3 green bell peppers, deseeded
1 green chili, deseeded
2 tbsp chopped fresh cilantro
2 scallions, finely chopped
1 tbsp crème fraîche or heavy cream
2 tbsp rice wine vinegar
1 tbsp sugar
¼ tsp Chinese mustard
• Place the peppers, chili, cilantro, and scallions in a small blender, mix to a coarse purée, remove to a bowl.
• Add the remaining ingredients, mix again, and leave to infuse for 1 hour or preferably overnight.

TO SERVE · 4 CRUSTY ROLLS OR BUNS, SPLIT · 8 GREEN BUTTER LETTUCE LEAVES
· HOT MANGO–CUCUMBER SALSA · COOL CHILI VERDE

Smoked-salmon burger bagel

with egg and caper relish, and quark and sweet mustard cream

Smoked salmon set on a lightly toasted bagel, topped with cream cheese, tiny sliced shallots, and capers is a classic Jewish specialty. Taking this theme I have created an alternative made from potato and smoked fish. It's easy to prepare and extremely healthy!

2 large potatoes, peeled
1 small onion, finely chopped
9 oz skinless, boneless white fish
  fillet (e.g. haddock, cod, halibut)
9 oz smoked salmon, coarsely
  chopped
salt and freshly ground black pepper
oil for cooking
flour for dusting

1 Using a grater, coarsely grate the potatoes and place in a cloth, then squeeze out the excess water. Place in a bowl, and add the onion.

2 Place the white fish and smoked salmon in a food processor with a little freshly ground black pepper. Mix quickly to a smooth paste, then remove and add to the potatoes and onion. Adjust the seasoning.

3 Shape into 4 evenly sized burgers.

4 Heat a nonstick frying pan and, when hot, add the oil to a depth of ½ inch. Dust the burgers lightly with flour, and fry them for 2–3 minutes each side, then remove and drain them on kitchen paper.

5 Toast the bagels and spread liberally with the quark and sweet mustard cream. Place some smoked salmon over, some baby spinach leaves, and top with the smoked salmon burger.

6 Spoon some egg and caper relish over, top with thinly sliced shallot rings, and serve.

TO SERVE • 4 FRESH BAGELS, SPLIT • 3 OZ SLICED SMOKED SALMON • BABY SPINACH LEAVES • 2 LARGE SHALLOTS, PEELED AND THINLY SLICED • QUARK AND SWEET MUSTARD CREAM • EGG AND CAPER RELISH

Quark and sweet mustard cream

1 tsp sweet mustard
1 small garlic clove, crushed
salt and freshly ground black
  pepper
½ cup quark cheese or other soft
  cheese (e.g ricotta or cream
  cheese)
2 tbsp chopped fresh dill
• Place the mustard, garlic, and a little seasoning in a bowl, mix well
• Beat in the quark until smooth and creamy.
• Add the dill, mix well, adjust the seasoning.

Egg and caper relish

½ tsp Dijon mustard
3 hard-boiled eggs, coarsely
  chopped
1 shallot, finely chopped
1 tbsp cocktail capers, coarsely
  chopped
1 tbsp chopped fresh flat-leaf
  parsley
¼ cup good quality French
  dressing
• Mix all together, leave to infuse for 30 minutes.

Tuna burger with cabbage tzatziki

Marcus Samuelsson originates from Sweden but lives in New York where he is chef at the Aquavit: one of the city's hottest restaurants—this recipe comes from his book *Aquavit: and the new Scandinavian cuisine.*

9 oz tuna steak, cut into ¼-inch dice
6 large sea scallops, cleaned, cut into
  ¼-inch dice
1 tbsp pickled ginger, finely chopped
2 garlic cloves, finely chopped
1 tbsp chopped fresh cilantro
1 tbsp Asian sweet chili sauce
1 tsp wasabi powder
¼ cup freshly squeezed lime juice
sea salt and freshly ground black pepper
olive oil for cooking

Cabbage tzatziki
1 cup plain Greek-style yogurt
3 garlic cloves
juice of 1 lime
2 tbsp chopped fresh dill
1 tbsp chopped fresh flat-leaf
  parsley
2 cups thinly sliced napa cabbage
  (Chinese cabbage)
sea salt
• Combine the yogurt, garlic, lime juice, dill and parsley in a food processor or blender and process until smooth.
• Put the cabbage in a bowl, add the yogurt mixture, toss to coat.
• Season with sea salt to taste.

1 In a medium bowl, combine the tuna, scallops, ginger, garlic, cilantro, chili sauce, wasabi, and lime juice, mixing well; season with salt and pepper. Let stand for 10 minutes, then transfer to a strainer, set over a bowl, to drain off any excess liquid.
2 Split the focaccia in half and toast lightly, brush the cut sides with a little of the olive oil.
3 Shape the tuna mixture in-to 4 patties. Heat some olive oil in a large frying pan over a medium-high heat until hot. Add the tuna burgers, reduce the heat to medium, and cook turning once, for 2 minutes on each side, or until golden brown. Take care not to overcook—the tuna should be medium-rare.
4 Put a slice of tomato on the bottom half of the squares of focaccia, top with the tuna burger, and spread the cabbage tzatziki over the tuna. Cover with the tops of the focaccia, and serve.

TO SERVE · 4 SMALL SQUARES FOCACCIA BREAD OR SMALL SOFT ROLLS · 4 SLICES TOMATO · CABBAGE TZATZIKI

Teriyaki-glazed tuna burger with shiso–seaweed salad

Another great-flavored tuna burger recipe to enjoy. I adore the salty, sweet Asian flavors which are both warm and delicately sweet. The seaweed can be purchased from Asian stores, usually salted, it needs to be soaked before use.

1 lb 8 oz fresh, skinless tuna steak
2 scallions, finely chopped
½ garlic clove, crushed
1 tsp Chinese or Dijon mustard
½-inch piece ginger root, grated
2 tbsp chopped fresh cilantro
salt and freshly ground black pepper
vegetable or sunflower oil for cooking

FOR THE GLAZE
¼ cup teriyaki sauce
2 tbsp honey
1-inch piece ginger root, grated
2 tsp rice wine vinegar

1 Cut the tuna into very small cubes or mix quickly in a food processor. Add the scallions, garlic, mustard, ginger, cilantro, and mix again briefly. Season lightly with salt and pepper. Transfer to a bowl and cover with plastic wrap, chill for 1 hour.

2 Mix all the ingredients for the glaze together in a bowl.

3 Divide the mix into 8 evenly sized burgers.

4 Heat a thin film of oil in a large nonstick frying pan and, when hot, add the burgers and cook for 3–4 minutes on each side, keeping them medium-rare, and brushing regularly with the glaze.

5 Toast the buns. Top the bases with the burgers, and then with the shiso–seaweed salad, close the buns and serve.

Shiso–seaweed salad
2 tbsp lime juice
½ small green chili, thinly sliced
1 tbsp sugar
1 tbsp light soy sauce
12 slices pickled ginger
½-inch piece ginger root, finely grated
1 tbsp chopped fresh cilantro
¼ cup peanut oil or vegetable oil
1 cup wakame seaweed, soaked in water for 2 hours, drained, dried
½ cup thinly sliced cucumber
2 scallions, thinly shredded lengthwise
½ cup frisee lettuce
½ cup shiso cress or mustard cress
salt and freshly ground black pepper

• In a bowl mix the lime juice, chili, sugar, soy sauce, ginger, and cilantro together. Add the oil and leave to infuse the flavors for 20 minutes.
• Place the seaweed, cucumber, and scallions in a bowl. Strain the dressing over, toss together well, and marinate for 1 hour at room temperature.
• To serve, add the frisee and shiso cress, toss lightly together, season and serve immediately.

TO SERVE • 8 MINI BURGER BUNS WITH BLACK SESAME SEEDS, SPLIT (SEE PAGE 135) • SHISO–SEAWEED SALAD

Piri piri tuna burger with grilled eggplant, spicy tomato relish, and almond picada

Piri piri chilies were brought to Portugal from the Americas. The Portuguese then took them to Mozambique where they were named piri piri—a Swahili name meaning 'pepper pepper'. They are very hot and need to be used sparingly.

1 lb 5 oz skinless, boneless yellow fin
  tuna steak
1 garlic clove, crushed
1 tsp piri piri sauce or hot pepper sauce
2 tbsp chopped fresh oregano
1 tbsp chopped fresh cilantro
2 tbsp olive oil
1 tsp freshly squeezed lemon juice
salt and freshly ground black pepper
pinch of paprika

1 Place the tuna steak in a food processor and mix to a coarse purée or chop by hand.
2 In a large bowl, place the tuna, garlic, pepper sauce, herbs, 1 tsp of the olive oil, and lemon juice; season with salt, pepper, and paprika, cover with plastic wrap and chill for 1 hour.
3 Divide the mix into 4 evenly sized burgers.
4 Heat the remaining olive oil in a large nonstick frying pan, add the burgers, and cook for 2 minutes on each side until golden brown. Take care not to overcook the tuna, it should be medium-rare.
5 Toast the buns, dress the bases with some salad leaves and 2 slices grilled eggplant. Place a dollop of spicy tomato relish on top, followed by the tuna burgers.
6 Finally, top each burger with almond picada, close the buns, and serve.

Grilled eggplant
¼ cup olive oil
1 large eggplant, cut into ½-inch-
  thick slices
sea salt and freshly ground black
  pepper
• Heat a pan grill with the olive oil,
when hot add the eggplant slices,
and grill for 3–4 minutes on each
side until soft and golden in color,
season to taste and serve.

Almond picada
1 garlic clove, peeled
¼ cup whole blanched almonds,
  lightly toasted
½ red chili, deseeded
¼ cup fresh flat-leaf parsley
¼ cup good quality mayonnaise
1 tsp freshly squeezed lemon
  juice
• Place the garlic clove, toasted
almonds, chili, and parsley in a
mortar and pestle, grind to a fine
paste.
• Add the mayonnaise, lemon juice,
season to taste, and serve.

TO SERVE • 4 BURGER BUNS, SPLIT • MIXED SALAD LEAVES • 8 SLICES GRILLED EGGPLANT • SPICY TOMATO RELISH (SEE PAGE 128) • ALMOND PICADA

Artichoke escalivada

2 red bell peppers, deseeded, cut into quarters
1 yellow pepper, deseeded, cut into quarters
½ eggplant, cut into ½-inch slices
⅓ cup olive oil
½ cup baby artichokes in oil, drained, halved
½ cup sundried tomatoes in oil, drained
1 tbsp balsamic vinegar
1 tbsp chopped fresh flat-leaf parsley
1 garlic clove, crushed
1 tsp lemon juice
1 tsp pine nuts, toasted

• Preheat a broiler at its highest setting. Arrange the peppers and eggplant slices on a broiler rack, drizzle with the olive oil, and broil until the skins are charred and tender.
• Remove the peppers to a bowl and cover with a plate or plastic wrap to steam for 5 minutes.
• Remove the cover and, when cool, peel them to remove the skins. Cut the peppers into strips.
• Place the pepper strips, eggplant slices and remaining ingredients in a bowl, toss together and serve.

Smoked paprika–sherry mayo

½ cup good quality mayonnaise (see page 126)
2 tsp smoked paprika or paprika
1 tsp sherry vinegar
pinch of salt

• Mix all the ingredients together, seasoning to taste.

Swordfish burger with artichoke escalivada, and smoked paprika–sherry mayo

Swordfish is identified with the Mediterranean, but it is becoming more widely available from fresh fish counters at good supermarkets. Like tuna, it is very nutritious and extremely lean. When cooking these burgers, do not let them get too hot or overcook or they become dry. Smoked paprika is available from Spanish delis.

1 lb 5 oz skinless, boneles, good quality fresh swordfish fillet
¼ cup ground almonds
juice and zest of ½ lemon
1 garlic clove, crushed
¼ cup good quality mayonnaise (page 126)
2 cups fresh white bread crumbs
salt, pinch of white cayenne
vegetable oil for cooking

TO COAT BURGERS
¼ cup all-purpose flour
1 egg, lightly beaten
1 cup panko crumbs or fresh white bread crumbs

1 Chop the swordfish finely, add the almonds, lemon juice and zest, and garlic. Add the mayonnaise and bread crumbs to bind. Season with salt and white cayenne to taste. Shape the mix into 8 evenly sized patties.
2 Coat the burgers: pass the patties through the flour, then the egg, and finally the panko crumbs. Chill for 30 minutes before cooking.
3 Heat a thin film of oil in a frying pan, suitable for the oven.
4 Cook the burgers gently for 4–5 minutes on each side, remove and drain on kitchen paper.
5 Toast the buns under a hot broiler until golden, if using.
6 Serve with artichoke escalivada, some patatas con ajo, and with a bowl of smoked paprika–sherry mayo on the side.

TO SERVE · 4 BURGER BUNS, SPLIT (OPTIONAL) · ARTICHOKE ESCALIVADA
· PATATAS CON AJO (SEE PAGE 139) · SMOKED PAPRIKA–SHERRY MAYO

TO SERVE · 4 BABY BAGUETTES OR SMALL CRUSTY ROLLS
· CREOLE RÉMOULADE SLAW (SEE PAGE 133)
· TWICE-COOKED JACKET POTATOES (SEE PAGE 139)

New Orleans po'boy with Creole rémoulade slaw, and twice-cooked jacket potatoes

7 oz skinless, boneless white fish fillet (e.g. cod, haddock or turbot), cut into chunks

1 lb tiger prawns, shelled, deveined

1 egg white

salt and freshly ground black pepper

3 scallions, finely chopped

2 tbsp chopped fresh basil

½ tsp Creole or Dijon mustard

1 tsp Worcestershire sauce

pinch of cayenne

vegetable or sunflower oil for cooking

1 Place the fish with 3½ oz of the prawns, the egg white, and a little salt in the food processor, and mix for 20 seconds

2 Add the scallions, basil, and mustard, then mix again for 5 seconds. Transfer to a bowl and mix in the Worcestershire sauce.

3 Chop the remaining tiger prawns in ¼-inch dice and add to the bowl. Adjust the seasoning with salt, pepper, and cayenne; chill in the refrigerator for 2 hours.

4 Using wet hands, divide the mix into 4 equal amounts and roll each into a ¾-inch-thick burger 5 inches in length, big enough to fill the baguettes.

5 Heat a chargrill or pan grill until hot, brush the grill with some oil. Add the burgers and grill for 4–5 minutes, turning them regularly until golden and cooked through.

6 Reheat the baby baguettes in the oven; slit down one side with a sharp knife and prize open the baguette, taking care not to split it.

7 Fill with the Creole rémoulade slaw and top with the fish burgers; serve with the twice-cooked jacket potatoes.

Cod burger bocadillo with tomato and olive pesto, and caper-saffron mayo

1 tbsp olive oil

2 shallots, finely chopped

14 oz skinless, boneless, firm white cod fillet

4 sea scallops

1 egg yolk

2 tbsp chopped fresh flat-leaf parsley

juice and zest of ¼ lemon

salt and freshly ground black pepper

pinch of paprika

flour for dusting

2 cups panko crumbs

vegetable or sunflower oil for cooking

2 tbsp unsalted butter

1 In a frying pan, heat the olive oil, add the shallots, and cook for 3–4 minutes until softened and tender; remove and allow to cool.

2 Place the shallots, cod fillet, scallop meat, egg yolk and parsley in a food processor. Add the lemon juice and zest, along with a little salt, pepper and paprika. Mix to a chunky paste—do not let it become too smooth—for about 20 seconds.

3 Using floured hands, divide the mix into 4 evenly sized burgers, then pass each burger through the beaten egg wash, then through the panko crumbs.

4 Pat into shape and to release any excess crumbs, chill for 30 minutes.

5 Heat a nonstick frying pan with a film of oil, add the burger and the butter, and fry for 4–5 minutes each side until golden and crisp.

6 Top the bases with the tomato and olive pesto, then top with a cod burger. Serve with some dressed salad, the caper–saffron mayo, and chickpea fries.

TO SERVE · 4 SMALL BAGUETTES OR ENGLISH MUFFINS, SPLIT · TOMATO AND OLIVE PESTO (SEE PAGE 126) · CRISP GREEN SALAD DRESSED IN FRENCH DRESSING · CAPER–SAFFRON MAYO (SEE PAGE 126) · CHICKPEA FRIES (SEE PAGE 140)

Olive couscous salad

½ cup couscous
⅔ cup hot chicken stock
½ yellow bell pepper, halved, deseeded, finely chopped
½ green bell pepper, halved, deseeded, finely chopped
1 garlic clove, crushed
⅔ cup pitted, chopped green olives
¼ cup olive oil
2 tbsp chopped fresh flat-leaf parsley
juice of ½ lemon
½ tsp ground cumin

• Place the couscous in a bowl, pour the chicken stock over, cover with plastic wrap, and leave for 5–6 minutes until the couscous swells.
• Uncover, fluff up with a fork, cover again, and leave for a further 5 minutes.
• Add the bell peppers, garlic, and olives to the couscous, mix well.
• Add the olive oil, parsley, lemon juice and cumin, toss well together and serve.

Jumbo prawn burger with North African spices, tomato chermoula, and olive couscous salad

In this recipe, marinating the fish really pays dividends, but ensure that the excess liquid is drained off or it will make the mix too soft. The traditional Moroccan chermoula is served with all manner of grilled foods, especially fish—this is a great variation.

12 oz skinless, boneless, white fish fillet (e.g. cod, haddock, halibut)
9 oz jumbo tiger prawns, shelled, deveined
1 small garlic clove, crushed
1 tsp freshly squeezed lemon juice
½ tsp ground cumin
¼ tsp sweet paprika
¼ tsp powdered saffron
¼ tsp ground ginger
1 egg, beaten
1 tbsp chopped fresh cilantro
1 tbsp chopped fresh flat-leaf parsley
salt and freshly ground black pepper
vegetable or sunflower oil for cooking

1 Cut the fish and prawns into large pieces, place in a bowl.
2 Add the garlic, lemon juice, cumin, paprika, saffron, and ginger and mix well; leave to marinate for 10 minutes.
3 Drain off any excess liquid, then place in a food processor and mix to a coarse paste. Transfer to a bowl, add the egg, herbs, salt and pepper, and mix well; chill for 1 hour.
4 Divide the mix into 8 evenly sized burgers.
5 Heat a thin film of oil in a large frying pan and, when hot, add the burgers and cook for 2–3 minutes on each side until golden. Remove and drain on kitchen paper.
6 Toast the buns. Mix the mayonnaise with the lettuce leaves, and place on the burger bases. Top with a burger, a few more leaves, then the second burger. Add a good dollop of tomato chermoula and close the lid. Serve with the olive couscous salad.

TO SERVE • 2 BURGER BUNS, SPLIT • ¼ CUP GOOD QUALITY MAYONNAISE
• 2 CUPS BABY RED CHARD LEAVES • TOMATO CHERMOULA • OLIVE COUSCOUS SALAD

Tomato chermoula

1 tsp cumin seeds
½ tsp coriander seeds
1 cup canned plum tomatoes
1 garlic clove, crushed
1 small red chili, deseeded, finely
  chopped
1 tbsp tomato purée
juice of ½ lemon
½ tsp ground sweet paprika

• Heat a dry frying pan over a high heat.
• Dry toast the cumin and coriander seeds for 10 seconds until they release their fragrance.
• Place in a mortar and pestle and crush until fine.
• Place in the blender, add the remaining ingredients and mix to a paste. Keep refrigerated until required.

Thai lobster and lemongrass sticks

with hot peanut–mint dip (makes 12)

These delicious little patties, cooked on their lemongrass sticks, really do make an
impressive talking point, served with Champagne of course! The perfect prelude to a meal.

14 lemongrass sticks
1 lb cleaned lobster or king prawns, deveined
4½ oz skinless, boneless white fish fillet
4 scallions
3 tbsp chopped fresh cilantro
1 tbsp Thai fish sauce (nam pla)
2 tsp honey
2 garlic cloves, crushed
1 small egg white
1 tsp cornstarch
1 tsp black sesame seeds
vegetable or sunflower oil for cooking

1 Remove the tough outer leaves of the lemongrass, chop 2 of them
   very finely; with the remaining 12, cut the tops off so that you
   have 6-inch lengths with the thickest part intact.
2 In a blender, place the lobster meat, white fish, chopped
   lemongrass, the remaining ingredients, and mix to a smooth paste.
3 Divide the mix into 12 x 1½-inch balls, using wet hands, then mold
   over the thick ends of the lemongrass sticks; chill in the refrigerator
   for 1 hour.
4 Sprinkle lightly with sesame seeds, then brush with a little oil; grill
   or panfry for 4–6 minutes, until golden. Serve the dip separately.

TO SERVE · HOT PEANUT–MINT DIP

Niçoise crab burger with fennel escabèche and sundried pepper rouille

14 oz skinless, boneless, firm white fish
   fillet (e.g. sole or halibut)
salt and freshly ground black pepper
7 oz freshly picked white crabmeat
2 tbsp good quality mayonnaise
2 tbsp freshly chopped flat-leaf parsley
¼ tsp Dijon mustard
zest of ¼ lemon
2 cups fresh white bread crumbs
vegetable or sunflower oil for cooking
2 tbsp unsalted butter

1 Place the white fish in a food processor with a little salt and mix to a coarse pulp. Transfer to a bowl and incorporate the crabmeat, mayonnaise, parsley, mustard, and lemon zest; mix well. Add the bread crumbs, mix again and season to taste.
2 Divide the mix into 4 evenly sized burgers.
3 Heat a thin film of oil in a nonstick frying pan, add the burgers and the butter and fry until golden and cooked through, about 4 minutes each side.
4 Cut the muffins in half, allowing half per person.
5 Place some fennel escabèche on each base, topped with the arugula leaves.
6 Place a burger on top, and garnish with a good dollop of sundried pepper rouille.

TO SERVE · 2 ENGLISH MUFFINS, SPLIT · ARUGULA LEAVES · FENNEL ESCABÈCHE · SUNDRIED PEPPER ROUILLE (SEE PAGE 125)

Fennel escabèche
1 large head fennel, peeled
2 tbsp lemon juice
⅓ cup olive oil
salt and freshly ground pepper
· Using a potato peeler, thinly shave or slice the fennel wafer thin. Place in a bowl, add the lemon juice, olive oil, salt and pepper, and leave to marinate for 4 hours before use.

Asian crab burger with sweet chili ketchup and yuzu crème fraîche

6 oz skinless, boneless white fish fillet
   (e.g. cod, haddock, etc.)
2 garlic cloves, crushed
1 tbsp Thai fish sauce (nam pla)
½ tbsp ketchup manis (Indonesian soy
   sauce)
½ tbsp oyster sauce
12 oz fresh white crabmeat
1 small egg, beaten
⅓ cup unsweetened, desiccated coconut
1 red chili, deseeded, finely chopped
4 scallions, thinly sliced
¼ cup chopped fresh cilantro
salt and freshly ground black pepper
vegetable or sunflower oil for cooking

1 Place the white fish fillet in a food processor, add the garlic, fish sauce, ketchup manis, oyster sauce, and process for a few seconds until it forms a coarse paste.
2 Dry the crabmeat on a cloth, squeeze out any excess moisture, and add to the fish. Add the egg and process once more.
3 Transfer the mixture to a bowl, add the coconut, chili, scallions, and cilantro. Season with salt and pepper.
4 Divide the mix into 8 evenly sized burgers. Heat a thin film of the oil in a frying pan, add the burgers and cook for 3–4 minutes until golden.
5 Toast the buns. Top the bases with shredded lettuce and slices of cucumber. Place some sweet chili ketchup on top, then top each with a burger. Repeat with a little more lettuce, cucumber, ketchup, then another burger. Finish with a dollop of yuzu crème fraîche, close the buns, and serve.

Yuzu crème fraîche
½ cup crème fraîche or heavy
   cream
3 tbsp bottled yuzu juice
   (available from Asian stores)
2 tbsp chopped fresh mint
1 tbsp chopped fresh cilantro
salt and freshly ground black
   pepper
• Mix all the ingredients together,
season to taste.

TO SERVE • BURGER BUNS, SPLIT • ½ CUP SHREDDED ICEBERG LETTUCE • ½ CUP THINLY
SLICED CUCUMBER • SWEET CHILI KETCHUP (SEE PAGE 125)

Deviled scallop burger with portobello mushrooms, mustard hollandaise, and thyme-grilled corn

I find that freshly caught scallop is the finest and most delicate of all molluscs. Scallops also make incredibly good and juicy burgers despite their low fat content. When cooking them take great care not to overcook them—the center should be barely cooked.

9 oz skinless, boneless lemon sole fillet
14 oz cleaned sea scallops
salt and freshly ground black pepper
½ cup fresh white bread crumbs
½ cup chopped fresh flat-leaf parsley
1 egg white
vegetable or sunflower oil for cooking
good pinch of cayenne

1 Place the lemon sole fillet in a food processor with half the scallops and a little salt. Add the bread crumbs and parsley and mix to a fine paste.

2 Take the remaining scallops and chop them roughly, add to the sole and process for 20 seconds or until just blended: there should be small lumps of scallops in the mixture. Add the egg white and mix, still keeping the mixture slightly chunky in texture. Season to taste with salt and pepper.

3 Using oiled hands, shape the mixture into burgers, place on a plate, cover, and refrigerate until ready to cook.

4 Heat a thin film of oil in a large nonstick frying pan and, when hot, remove the burgers from the refrigerator and dust them all over with a little cayenne pepper.

5 Cook the burgers for 4–5 minutes on each side until golden; they should remain a little undercooked in the center to keep them juicy and moist.

6 Place the grilled portobello mushrooms on 4 serving plates, top each with a slice of tomato, and then with a scallop burger.

7 Coat each burger with some mustard hollandaise, garnish with watercress, grilled bacon, and thyme-grilled corn.

Grilled portobello mushrooms

3 tbsp vegetable oil
4 portobello mushrooms, stems removed, peeled
salt and freshly ground black pepper

• Heat a pan or chargrill until hot, brush with the vegetable oil, and cook the mushrooms for 6–8 minutes until charred all over; season to taste.

Mustard hollandaise

⅓ cup white wine vinegar
1 tsp crushed black peppercorns
4 egg yolks
⅔ cup unsalted butter, clarified, hot
juice of ¼ lemon
2 tsp Dijon mustard

• Place the vinegar in a small pan with 2 tbsp cold water and the peppercorns. Bring to a boil for 30 seconds, then strain into a heatproof bowl, cool slightly.
• Place the bowl over a pan of boiling water, and whisk in the egg yolks until they double in volume and become opaque in color.
• Add the hot clarified butter in a thin stream and whisk until thickened. Add the lemon juice and mustard and keep the sauce warm, but do not let it get too hot or the sauce will separate.

Thyme-grilled corn

3 corn cobs, husks removed
¼ cup vegetable oil
⅓ cup unsalted butter
2 tsp freshly picked thyme leaves
salt and freshly ground black pepper

• Blanch the corn in boiling water for 10 minutes, remove, and cut in 1½-inch chunks.
• Brush with the oil, heat a chargrill or grill pan until hot, grill for 10 minutes until lightly charred, turning them often.
• Heat the butter with the thyme in a pan for 2 minutes, pour over the grilled corn, season, and serve.

TO SERVE • GRILLED PORTOBELLO MUSHROOMS • 4 THICK SLICES LARGE TOMATOES • MUSTARD HOLLANDAISE
• ½ CUP WATERCRESS • 8 SLICES BACON, GRILLED • THYME-GRILLED CORN

Walnut, zucchini,
and millet burger

Walnut, zucchini, and millet burger
with lemon mint labna and smoky tomato and bell-pepper relish

1 zucchini, grated
salt and freshly ground black pepper
½ tsp curry powder
⅛ tsp turmeric
⅔ cup millet
2 tbsp vegetable oil
1 onion, finely chopped
1 cup finely chopped flat mushrooms
1¼ cups finely ground walnuts
1 cup fresh white bread crumbs
1 egg, beaten

Lemon mint labna
1 egg white
½ cup Greek-style yogurt, thick variety or
  well drained
zest of ¼ lemon
· Whisk the egg white until stiff, then fold in the
yogurt to combine, add the lemon zest,
seasoning lightly, and serve.

1 Place the grated zucchini on a tray, sprinkle liberally with salt, and leave for 25 minutes to extract the moisture. Rinse under cold water, squeeze dry in your hands, and dry in a cloth.
2 In a pan, bring 1¼ cups water to a boil with the curry, turmeric, and a little salt. Add the millet, simmer gently for 15–20 minutes over a low heat, until the millet has absorbed all the water. Transfer to a bowl, leave to go cold.
3 Heat the oil in a nonstick frying pan, add the onion, and cook until soft and tender. Add the grated zucchini and mushroom, and cook for 5 minutes until soft.
4 In a bowl, mix the ground walnuts, cooked millet, bread crumbs with the vegetables. Add the beaten egg and mix to a paste. Season with pepper to taste.
5 Place in the refrigerator to chill for 1 hour, then shape into 4 evenly sized burgers.
6 Lay some dressed salad leaves on the half potatoes, top with some smoky bell-pepper relish. Place a burger on each, then top with a good dollop of lemon mint labna, close with the potato lid, and serve.

TO SERVE · 4 JACKET POTATOES, SPLIT · MIXED SALAD LEAVES, DRESSED IN FRENCH DRESSING · SMOKY TOMATO AND BELL-PEPPER RELISH (SEE PAGE 130) · LEMON MINT LABNA

Vegetarian feta club burger with cilantro–avocado pesto and slow-dried tomatoes

1 onion, firmly chopped
1 cup crumbled feta cheese
1 tbsp chopped fresh mint
2 cups fresh white bread crumbs
3 tbsp chickpea flour (gram flour)
1 large egg
salt and freshly ground black pepper
vegetable or sunflower oil for cooking

Cilantro–avocado pesto
2 cups picked fresh cilantro leaves
1 garlic clove, crushed
1 avocado, stone removed
2 tbsp freshly grated Parmesan cheese
2 tbsp pine nuts, toasted
½ cup extra-virgin olive oil
· Place the cilantro leaves and garlic in a
blender, add the avocado flesh, Parmesan, and
pine nuts, and mix to a purée; using the feed
tube at the top of the blender, slowly drizzle in
the olive oil to form a sauce. Season to taste.

1 Place the onion in a bowl, add the crumbled feta, mint, bread crumbs, and chickpea flour. Add the egg, season to taste, and bind together; chill the mix for 30 minutes, then shape into 8 small, fairly flat-shaped burgers.
2 Heat a film of oil in a nonstick frying pan, add the burgers and fry gently for 3–4 minutes on each side, remove and keep them warm.
3 Take 4 slices of the sour dough bread, and spread liberally with the olive mayo. Top each with some iceberg and arugula leaves, followed by a burger.
4 Top with slow-dried tomatoes, a layer of sliced egg, then a good dollop of the cilantro–avocado pesto.
5 Top with a second slice of bread and repeat the layers again.
6 Finish with the last slice of bread, then press gently down to compress the filling within. Cut into 2 halves and enjoy!

TO SERVE · 12 THIN SLICES SOUR DOUGH BREAD · ICEBERG LETTUCE · ½ CUP ARUGULA LEAVES · SLOW-DRIED TOMATOES · 2 HARD-BOILED EGGS, SHELLED, SLICED · OLIVE MAYO (SEE PAGE 126) · CILANTRO–AVOCADO PESTO

Slow-dried tomatoes

8 ripe but firm plum tomatoes,
  cut in half horizontally
1 garlic clove, crushed
1 tbsp picked fresh thyme
  leaves
½ tsp castor sugar
coarse sea salt, freshly ground
  pepper
¼ cup olive oil

• Preheat the oven to 400°F.
Place the tomatoes on a baking
tray, cut-side up, scatter over
and rub on the garlic, thyme
leaves, sugar, salt, and pepper.
• Finally, drizzle the oil over,
place in the oven to bake until
very soft and shriveled. Leave to
cool. These keep in olive oil for
up to a week in the refrigerator.

Grilled eggplant, goat cheese, and sundried-tomato burger

This recipe is from talented chef and friend Peter Gordon, the man said to have brought 'fusion' cooking to Britain. Peter is consultant to Gourmet Burger Kitchen, a themed burger restaurant group serving wonderful burger creations throughout London; he recommends using sour dough buns if you can find them.

4 x ½-inch slices firm chèvre (goat cheese) log
3 tbsp flour
salt and freshly ground black pepper
1 egg, beaten for egg wash
1 cup panko crumbs mixed with 1 tbsp honey
vegetable or sunflower oil for deep frying
8 x ½-inch-thick slices eggplant
olive oil for brushing

1 Coat the goat cheese slices as follows: dust the slices of cheese with the flour, mixed with a little salt and pepper. Dip them in to the egg wash and then into the panko crumbs.
2 Press the panko into the goat cheese firmly. Dip again into the egg wash and then again into the panko. It is important to double coat to prevent the cheese oozing into the fryer oil. Chill in the refrigerator for at least 30 minutes.
3 Heat the oil in a deep-fat fryer or large saucepan to 350°F.
4 Heat a cast iron pan grill until very hot, brush the eggplant slices with olive oil, and grill them until cooked to a golden color, about 3 minutes each side.
5 Fry the goat cheese burgers for 3–4 minutes until golden, then drain well on kitchen paper. Toast the burger buns on both sides.
6 Assemble the burgers: spread the bun bases with the mayonnaise, then top each with 2 slices of eggplant, then with the sundried tomatoes.
7 Place a goat cheese burger on top, then the cooked tomato relish, a few salad leaves dressed in a little balsamic vinaigrette, and close the lid. If you like, serve with long satay sticks to keep them from toppling over. Serve with more relish alongside.

Balsamic vinaigrette
1 tbsp balsamic vinegar
¼ cup extra-virgin olive oil
salt and freshly ground black pepper
• Whisk ingredients together and serve.

TO SERVE • 4 PLAIN OR SOUR DOUGH BURGER BUNS, SPLIT (PAGE 135)
• ½ CUP SUNDRIED TOMATOES IN OIL, DRAINED • 1 CUP MIXED SALAD LEAVES • BALSAMIC VINAIGRETTE • ¼ CUP GOOD QUALITY MAYONNAISE
• ¼ CUP COOKED TOMATO RELISH (SEE PAGE 129)

Pumpkin couscous burger in pitas with pomegranate–herb chili yogurt

In this burger recipe the squash adds a nutty sweetness and, when mixed with delicate spices and fluffy couscous, makes an interesting flavor-packed veggie burger. Prepare this wonderful yogurt-based dip to serve when pomegranates are available!

10-oz wedge pumpkin or butternut squash
1 large potato, washed
1 cup couscous, cooked to package
   instructions
¾ cup currants
1 onion, finely chopped
¾ cup finely chopped walnuts
2 tsp ground cumin
1 tsp ground cinnamon
1 tsp ground allspice
2 eggs, beaten

1 Preheat the oven to 400°F.
2 Place the pumpkin and the potato on a baking tray and place in the oven to bake. Remove the pumpkin after 30 minutes, leave the potato for a further 30 minutes or longer, depending on the size of the potato.
3 When both are cooked, allow to cool. Peel the potato and remove the skin from the pumpkin. Place the flesh in a large bowl, and mash to a coarse purée.
4 Add the couscous, currants, onion, walnuts, and spices, and bind together with the eggs. Shape the mix into 8 x 4-inch sausage-like burgers.
5 Cook the burgers on a chargrill or in a nonstick frying pan until cooked and golden.
6 Open up the pita breads, fill each with shredded lettuce, cucumber slices, and 2 pumpkin burgers. Serve the pomegranate–herb chili yogurt on the side.

Pomegranate–herb chili yogurt
⅔ cup natural thick-set Greek-style yogurt
3 scallions, finely chopped
1 green chili, finely chopped
½ garlic clove, crushed
1 tsp white wine vinegar
salt
1 tbsp chopped fresh dill
1 tbsp chopped fresh mint
1 fresh pomegranate, halved, seeds
   removed
1 tbsp pomegranate molasses (optional)
• If the yogurt is not thick you will have to line a colander with cheesecloth, place over a bowl, add the yogurt, and let it drain for at least 5 minutes, preferably overnight.
• In a bowl, mix the thick yogurt with the scallions, chili, garlic and vinegar, season with salt. Add the herbs. Squeeze out the seeds from the pomegranate halves and add them with the molasses, if using.
• Serve chilled.

TO SERVE · 8 FRESHLY BAKED MINI PITA BREADS (SEE PAGE 135)
· SHREDDED ICEBERG LETTUCE · CUCUMBER SLICES
· POMEGRANATE–HERB CHILI YOGURT

Roasted vegetable and kasha falafel burger with smoky corn relish

You'll find kasha (roasted buckwheat groats) in most health food stores—I love kasha made into falafel-style burgers and even big meat lovers will find they make vegetarian eating a real pleasure. Char the corn on the grill for a wonderful smoky relish.

⅔ cup whole grain kasha (roasted buckwheat groats)

1 egg

1 tbsp unsalted butter

1 onion, finely diced

1 carrot, peeled, finely diced

1 zucchini, finely diced

2 garlic cloves, crushed

3 cups cooked chickpeas (canned are fine, well drained)

2 scallions, finely chopped

2 tbsp chopped fresh cilantro

2 tbsp plain flour

2 tsp ground cumin

¼ tsp baking powder

salt, freshly ground black pepper

cayenne pepper

vegetable oil for deep frying

1 Place the kasha and egg in a small bowl, leave to stand for 10 minutes.

2 Melt the butter in a frying pan over moderate heat. Add the vegetables and garlic and fry for 8 minutes until soft. Add the kasha and fry for 3–4 minutes until the kasha is golden.

3 Add 1¼ cups water, bring to a boil, season with a little salt, cover and simmer for 15–20 minutes until the kasha is tender and all the water is absorbed, remove and cool.

4 To make the falafel, place the kasha, vegetables, and remaining ingredients in a blender and mix to form a moist paste, season to taste. Form into 8 x 2-inch-diameter patties.

5 Place the vegetable oil in a deep-fat fryer or deep saucepan and heat to 350°F. Fry the kasha falafel in batches until golden brown, about 2 minutes; drain on kitchen paper and keep them warm.

6 Toast the burger buns, place a good dollop of corn relish on the base bun, followed by a falafel burger, some salad leaves, and a slice of beet. Finish with the remaining falafel burger and close the lid. Serve the lemon mint labna alongside.

Smoky corn relish

3 corn cobs, husks removed

¾ cup white wine vinegar

⅓ cup sugar

1 garlic clove, crushed

1-inch piece ginger root, finely grated

½ tsp ground allspice

¼ tsp dried mustard powder

4 scallions, white part only, finely chopped

1 red bell pepper, halved, deseeded, finely chopped

1 small red chili, deseeded, finely chopped

1 tsp cornstarch mixed with 1 tsp of cold water

salt and freshly ground black pepper

• Blanch the corn in boiling water for 2–3 minutes, remove, and drain.

• Heat a chargrill or pan grill until very hot. Add the corn and grill for 5–6 minutes, turning them, until lightly charred all over.

• When cool enough to handle, run a small knife along the length of the corn to remove the kernels.

• In a pan, bring to a boil the vinegar, sugar, and the garlic, ginger, and spices, cook for 10–15 minutes.

• Add the corn kernels, scallions, bell pepper, and chili, and cook for a further 6–8 minutes. Stir in the cornstarch, cook for 30 seconds, season to taste, and cool.

• Refrigerate for at least 2 days before serving; it will keep in the refrigerator for up to 5 days.

TO SERVE · 4 SESAME BURGER BUNS, SPLIT · ½ CUP GREEN SALAD LEAVES · 4 THICK SLICES COOKED BEETS
· SMOKY CORN RELISH · ½ CUP LEMON MINT LABNA (SEE PAGE 106)

The spa burger with mango–alfalfa sprouts, and red bell-pepper and cashew tarator

I created this burger for the spa complex at the Lanesborough hotel, London, to serve to guests as they were being pampered. Cottage cheese, spinach, and wheatgerm, offset by a nutty bell-pepper sauce and delicate alfalfa sprouts, tempts the most jaded palates.

olive oil for frying
1 onion, finely chopped
1 garlic clove, crushed
½ cup cooked spinach
½ cup cottage cheese, well drained
2 cups fresh white bread crumbs
½ cup wheatgerm, lightly toasted
½ cup ground walnuts
2 tbsp chopped fresh mint
1 egg
salt and freshly ground black pepper
pinch of cayenne

1 Heat a little oil in a nonstick frying pan, add the onion, garlic, and cook until softened.
2 Squeeze the cooked spinach in a clean cloth to remove all the excess moisture, then chop it and add to the pan. Transfer the contents of the pan to a bowl, add the remaining ingredients, binding with the egg. Season to taste.
3 Divide the mix into 4 evenly sized burgers.
4 Heat a thin film of the oil in a nonstick frying pan, add the burgers, and cook for 3–4 minutes on each side until golden.
5 Toast the burger buns, spread some red bell-pepper and cashew tarator on the bases, then top with the burgers. Finally add a heap of alfalfa sprout slaw on top, close the bun, and serve with a fresh green salad.

TO SERVE · 4 SESAME BURGER BUNS, SPLIT · MANGO–ALFALFA SPROUTS · RED BELL-PEPPER AND CASHEW TARATOR · GREEN SALAD

Mango–alfalfa sprouts
1½ cups alfalfa sprouts
1 mango, finely shredded
1 cup fresh cilantro leaves
2 tbsp maple syrup
1 small red onion, thinly sliced
2 tbsp olive oil
juice of 1 lime
· Toss all the ingredients together just before serving.

Red bell-pepper and cashew tarator
1¼ cups fresh white bread crumbs
⅓ cup skimmed milk
¼ cup roasted red bell peppers in oil, drained, oil reserved
½ cup cashew nuts
2 garlic cloves, crushed
salt and freshly ground black pepper
· Place the bread crumbs in a bowl, pour the milk over, and leave to soak for 10 minutes.
· Place the peppers, cashew nuts, and garlic in a blender and mix to a smooth purée.
· Squeeze out any excess moisture from the bread, add to the blender, and mix again.
· Finally add 1 tbsp of the drained pepper oil. Season to taste. The tarator should be fairly thick in consistency, if not, add a little more bread crumbs.

Black bean koftas with corn and grilled-pineapple mojo

¼ cup vegetable oil

3 scallions, finely chopped

1 garlic clove, crushed

1 small green chili, deseeded, finely
   chopped

1½ cups cooked black beans

2 tsp Dijon mustard

2 tsp chickpea flour (gram flour)

¼ cup chopped fresh cilantro

½ tsp ground cumin

1½ cups fresh white bread crumbs

salt and freshly ground black pepper

1 cup feta cheese or other sharp cheese,
   cut into ½-inch dice

1 Heat 2 tbsp of the oil in a pan, add the scallions, garlic, and chili. Cook for 2 minutes.
2 Mash the cooked beans with the mustard, chickpea flour, cilantro, and cumin, and mix well.
   Add the bread crumbs and cooked onion mix. Season to taste.
3 Shape the mix into 1¼-inch balls. With your finger make a small indentation in the center of
   each ball, then fill each with some cheese. Cover over to secure the cheese filling.
4 Heat the remaining oil and fry the koftas for 3—4 minutes, keeping them moving.
5 Serve the cooked koftas in the prepared corn husks with the corn and grilled-pineapple mojo,
   garnished with fresh cilantro leaves.

TO PREPARE THE CORN HUSKS
   Soak the corn husks in hot water for 2 hours or until soft and pliable. Shake off the excess
   water. Take each husk and tear two thin strips off lengthwise to make the ties. Roll up the
   larger part and fasten a tie ½ inch from each end with a tight bow. Carefully open the center
   to form a little boat shape.

TO SERVE • 4 DRIED CORN HUSKS (SEE ABOVE)
• CORN AND GRILLED-PINEAPPLE MOJO (SEE PAGE 131)
• FRESH CILANTRO LEAVES TO GARNISH

Turkistan chickpea burger with pistachio, beet, and feta tabbouleh

2 tbsp olive oil
1 small onion, finely chopped
1 garlic clove, crushed
1 tsp ground cumin
½ cup cracked wheat (bulgur), soaked in boiling water for 20 minutes, then well drained
1 tbsp chopped fresh flat-leaf parsley
1¾ cup cooked chickpeas (canned are fine)
¾ cup freshly grated cheddar cheese
3 tbsp pine nuts, toasted
salt and freshly ground black pepper
vegetable or sunflower oil for cooking

TO SERVE · 8 MINI PITA BREADS (SEE PAGE 135)
· PISTACHIO, BEET, AND FETA TABBOULEH (SEE PAGE 133)

1 Heat the olive oil in a frying pan, add the onion, garlic, and cumin, and cook for 6–8 minutes until soft.
2 Add the cracked wheat and parsley and cook for 5 minutes longer.
3 Transfer to a food processor, add the remaining ingredients, and mix to a coarse paste.
4 Using wet hands, shape the mix into 4 evenly sized burgers, chill for 1 hour.
5 Heat a chargrill or pan grill with a little oil and, when hot, add the burgers and cook gently for 3–4 minutes each side.
6 Chargrill the pita breads. Serve the burgers between the hot pita breads and with the pistachio, beet, and feta tabbouleh alongside.

Lentil nut koftas with rojal salsa, and cumin naan bread

Indian cooking is renowned for its earthy lentil-based dishes. These lentil nut koftas are delicately spiced and made from the best Puy lentils. Everyone will adore them, especially when served with the fragrant sweet and sour rojal salsa. Utterly delicious!

Rojal salsa
1 tomato, chopped
1 shallot, cut into thin rings
2 scallions, chopped
¼ cup fresh pineapple, chopped
¼ cup cucumber, chopped
2 tbsp peanut oil
2 tbsp maple syrup
1 tbsp lime pickle, chopped
1 tbsp unsweetened desiccated coconut
salt and freshly ground black pepper
· Mix all the ingredients together in a bowl and leave to infuse for 1 hour before use.

Cilantro raita
½ cup plain yogurt
2 tbsp chopped fresh cilantro
pinch of saffron
Mix all the ingredients together, ready for use.

TO SERVE · 8 CUMIN NAAN BREADS (SEE PAGE 136)
· ROJAL SALSA · CILANTRO RAITA · MINT LEAVES TO GARNISH

¼ cup vegetable oil
1 onion
2 garlic cloves, crushed
1 green chili, deseeded, finely chopped
1 tsp ground coriander
¼ tsp black mustard seeds
14 oz cooked Puy lentils
1 tbsp curry paste
½ cup ground almonds
⅓ cup salted almonds
1 small egg
¼ cup chickpea flour (gram flour)
salt and freshly ground black pepper
8 bamboo or wooden skewers, soaked

1 Preheat the broiler to its highest setting.
2 Heat 1½ inches of oil in a frying pan and, when hot, add the onion, garlic, chili, ground coriander, and mustard seeds, cook for 2–3 minutes until the onion is soft and lightly golden.
3 Add the cooked lentils and cook for a further 2–3 minutes.
4 Add the curry paste and cook for a further 2 minutes.
5 Transfer to a food processor, add the almonds, egg, and 3 tbsp of the flour, and pulse until the mix comes together firmly. Season to taste.
6 Using 8 pre-soaked bamboo skewers and floured hands, mold the mix around the skewers to form a kofta sausage shape, ½–1 inch thick. Place on a broiler tray, brush with the remaining oil, and broil until golden, about 5 minutes, turning them regularly. Alternatively pan fry them in a nonstick pan.
7 Garnish the kofta burgers with mint leaves, and serve on the warm cumin naan breads, with bowls of rojal salsa and cilantro raita alongside.

Quorn bruschetta with Moroccan-style caponata

vegetable or sunflower oil for cooking

1 onion, finely chopped

1 garlic clove, crushed

1-inch piece root ginger, peeled, finely grated

½ tsp ground cumin

scant ½ cup almonds

1 cup fresh white bread crumbs

10 oz quorn mince

1 large egg

1 tbsp heavy cream

2 tbsp chopped fresh cilantro

1 tbsp chopped fresh mint

salt and freshly ground black pepper

1 Heat a thin film of the oil in a nonstick frying pan, and add the onion, garlic, ginger, and cumin; cook until soft, about 3–4 minutes, then add the almonds and bread crumbs and cook for a further 2 minutes.

2 Transfer the mixture to a food processor, add the quorn mince and egg, and mix to a coarse purée. Transfer to a bowl, add the cream, chopped cilantro, and mint. Season to taste.

3 Divide the mix into 4 evenly sized burgers.

4 Heat a thin film of oil in a nonstick frying pan, add the burgers, fry until golden on both sides and crisp.

5 Split the baguette in half lengthwise and toast, top with some dressed salad leaves, then top each with some Moroccan-style caponata and a quorn burger, and serve immediately.

Moroccan-style caponata

¼ tsp cumin seeds

¼ cup olive oil

1 stalk celery, peeled, thickly sliced

½ eggplant, cut into ½-inch dice

1 small red bell pepper, halved, deseeded, cut into ½-inch dice

1 onion, chopped

1 zucchini cut in ½-inch dice

8 green olives, pitted

1 garlic clove, crushed

¼ tsp paprika

¼ tsp ground cinnamon

2 tbsp balsamic vinegar

2 tbsp maple syrup

2 tbsp soaked raisins

• Heat a dry frying pan over a high heat, add the cumin seeds and quickly toast them to give off their fragrance. Remove.

• Add the oil to the pan, add the vegetables, olives, and garlic, and fry for 6–8 minutes until slightly softened. Add the spices, the cumin seeds, and cook for a further 2 minutes.

• Add the vinegar, syrup, and raisins; cover, reduce the heat, and cook until the vegetables are tender and syrupy.

• The caponata can be served cold or hot. I suggest hot for this burger. The caponata can be made up to 3 days in advance.

TO SERVE · 1 X 5-INCH LENGTH BAGUETTE · GREEN SALAD LEAVES, DRESSED IN BALSAMIC DRESSING · MOROCCAN-STYLE CAPONATA

Southwest red-bean burger with green chili mayo, and three-onion ceviche

1 tbsp olive oil
1 onion, finely chopped
1 garlic clove, crushed
1 tsp ground cumin
1 tsp ground coriander
¼ tsp turmeric
1½ cups finely chopped portobello mushrooms
1¾ cups cooked or canned red kidney beans
2 tbsp chopped fresh cilantro
2 cups crushed spicy tortilla chips
1¼ cups fresh white bread crumbs
1 tbsp hot pepper sauce
salt and freshly ground black pepper
flour for dusting
vegetable oil for cooking

1 Heat the oil in a frying pan, add the onion and garlic, and cook until softened. Add the spices, mix well, and cook for a further 2 minutes. Add the mushrooms, and cook over a low heat until they are soft but dry.
2 Place the beans in a bowl and mash lightly with a fork; add to the mushrooms along with the cilantro, crushed tortilla chips, bread crumbs, and pepper sauce. Season to taste.
3 Using floured hands, form the mixture into 4 evenly sized burgers (if the mix is a little too wet, add more bread crumbs). Brush the burgers with a little oil.
4 Heat a thin film of the oil in a large nonstick frying pan and, when hot, add the burgers. Cook for 2–3 minutes on each side until golden and crispy.
5 Toast the buns and top the bases with 2 slices of tomato, then a good dollop of green chili mayonnaise, followed by a burger. Finish with the three-onion ceviche and close the bun.

Three-onion ceviche

juice of 1 lime
2 tbsp peanut oil
½ garlic clove, crushed
1 tbsp chopped fresh cilantro
4 scallions, in 2-inch lengths, shredded
1 red onion, halved, thinly sliced
2 tbsp chives, in 2-inch lengths

salt and freshly ground black pepper
• In a bowl, whisk together the lime juice, peanut oil, and garlic, and add the cilantro. Leave to marinate for 30 minutes. Just before serving, add the scallions, onion, and chives, and toss gently together. Season to taste.

TO SERVE • 4 CHEESE BURGER BUNS, SPLIT (SEE PAGE 135)• 8 SLICES TOMATO • THREE-ONION CEVICHE • GREEN CHILI MAYO (SEE PAGE 126)

Oven cheese fries

Sauces

Simple tomato ketchup

Simple tomato ketchup

2 tbsp olive oil
2 onions, peeled, finely chopped
2 garlic cloves, crushed
4 x 14-oz cans peeled plum tomatoes, chopped
1⅓ cup light brown sugar
⅔ cup cider or white wine vinegar
2 tbsp tomato purée
2 tbsp black treacle or molasses
2 tsp dried mustard powder
2-inch piece cinnamon stick
½ tsp ground coriander
¼ tsp dried chili flakes
¼ tsp ground cloves
1 small bayleaf
juice of 2 limes

• Heat the oil in a heavy based pan, add the onions, garlic, and cook for 5–6 minutes until softened but with no color. Add all the remaining ingredients except the lime juice and bring to a boil.
• Reduce the heat to low and simmer the ketchup for 1–1¼ hours, stirring frequently.
• Pass the ketchup sauce through a medium strainer or food mill and return it to the pan.
• Cook over a low heat again for a further 30 minutes or so until the sauce is reduced and thickened in consistency.
• Allow to cool before stirring in the lime juice. Refrigerate until needed, it can be kept in a sealed container in the refrigerator for up to 5 days, longer in a sealed, sterilized jar.

PAUL GAYLER VARIATIONS

HORSERADISH KETCHUP
Add 1 tbsp freshly grated horseradish to the recipe during cooking.

CURRY KETCHUP
Add 2 tbsp curry paste to the cooked onion and garlic, cook for 5 minutes before adding the remaining ingredients.

SWEET CHILI KETCHUP
Add 2 tbsp Asian sweet chili sauce to the finished ketchup.

TABASCO–CUMIN KETCHUP
Replace the ground coriander in the recipe with 2 tbsp toasted and crushed cumin seeds, finish the ketchup with Tabasco sauce to taste.

Green tomato ketchup

A great way of using that glut of green tomatoes, both tasty and very economical, kept sterilized, it keeps for months and makes a refreshing change from the deep red variety.

6½ lb green tomatoes, roughly chopped
⅓ cup sea salt or coarse salt
2 tbsp olive oil
4 onions, peeled, finely chopped
3 garlic cloves, crushed
4½ cups brown sugar
2¾ cups white wine vinegar or cider vinegar
2 tsp ground turmeric
1 tsp mustard seed
1 tsp celery seed
1 tsp ground ginger
1 tsp black peppercorns, finely crushed
1 tsp ground coriander

• Place the tomatoes in a large bowl, sprinkle with salt, and leave to stand for 1 hour to release juices.
• Heat the oil in a heavy based saucepan, add the onions and garlic, and cook for 5–6 minutes without coloring.
• Rinse the tomatoes under fresh cold water, drain well, and add to the pan. Add all the remaining ingredients, and bring to a boil.
• Reduce the heat and simmer for 1 hour or until very soft and pulpy in consistency.
• Pass the mixture through a medium strainer or food mill, then return to the pan.
• Cook for a further 35 minutes until the tomatoes are reduced and thickened.
• Allow to cool and refrigerate until needed. To store longer, place the green tomato ketchup in a hot, sterilized preserving jar.

Sun-dried bell-pepper rouille

1 baking potato
¼ cup olive oil
1 garlic clove, crushed
⅓ cup sundried red bell peppers, chopped
1 egg yolk
salt and freshly ground black pepper
good pinch of cayenne

• Preheat the oven to 350°F.
• Place the potato on a baking tray, and bake in the oven for 1–1¼ hours or until soft; remove and cool slightly.
• Meanwhile warm the olive oil and garlic in a small pan, stir in the bell peppers, remove from the heat, and leave to soften for 10–15 minutes.
• Cut the potato in half, then using a spoon, scoop out the inner flesh into a blender.
• Add the bell peppers and garlic oil and mix to a thick purée. Finally add the egg yolk, salt and pepper, and the cayenne to give a little heat.

Beb's barbecue sauce

3 lb yellow onions, cut in several large pieces
3 green bell peppers, seeded, cut into several large pieces
1 bunch celery, cut into large lengths
leaves from 1 bunch fresh parsley
1 bunch scallion tops
1 head garlic, separated into cloves and peeled
8 cups vegetable oil
3 x 8-oz cans tomato sauce
½ cup bottled ketchup
1¼ cups Worcestershire sauce
3 tbsp yellow mustard
3 tbsp sugar
3 tbsp salt
½ cup unsalted butter
¼ cup Tabasco sauce

• Place the onions, bell peppers, celery, parsley, scallions tops, and garlic in a food processor until finely ground.
• Combine the ground vegetables with the oil, tomato sauce, ketchup, Worcestershire sauce, mustard, sugar, salt, butter, and Tabasco in a large heavy pot and stir to mix. Cook stirring often over a low heat for about 1½ hours.
• Remove from the heat and let cool, skim the oil that rises to the surface, and reserve.
• Store the sauce and the oil in airtight containers for up to 2 days in the refrigerator, or in the freezer for up to 3 months.
• Reheat before using.

My barbecue sauce

2 tbsp lard or vegetable oil
1 onion, roughly chopped
1 garlic clove, crushed
1 tsp paprika
1 cup tomato ketchup (see left)
⅔ cup tomato juice
3 tbsp Worcestershire sauce
2 tbsp black treacle
1 tbsp cider or white wine vinegar
2 tsp Dijon mustard
1 tsp hot pepper sauce or Tabasco

• Heat the lard or oil in a pan and, when hot, add the onion and garlic, and cook for 5 minutes until soft and tender.
• Add the paprika and cook for a further 2 minutes.
• Add the remaining ingredients and bring to a boil; reduce the heat and cook for 30 minutes until reduced and thickened in consistency.
• Remove and allow to cool, ready for use.

Basil pesto

Olive mayo

Green harissa mayo

Basil pesto

2 cups fresh basil leaves
½ cup finely grated Parmigiano Reggiano cheese
2 tbsp pine nuts
2 garlic cloves, peeled
2 tbsp extra-virgin olive oil
salt and freshly ground black pepper

• Place the basil, Parmesan, pine nuts, and garlic in a liquidizer or food processor and mix until almost a paste.
• While the motor is running, slowly add the oil through the feed tube at the top, until the pesto sauce is thick and slightly coarse in texture. Season to taste, ready for use.

Tomato and olive pesto

2 garlic cloves, peeled
12 basil leaves
salt and freshly ground black pepper
½ cup sundried tomatoes in oil, drained, oil reserved
1 tbsp chopped black olives
1 tbsp grated Parmigiano Reggiano cheese

• Crush the garlic and basil in a mortar and pestle with a little salt until it becomes a paste. Chop the sundried tomatoes in small pieces and place in a bowl with the olives and Parmesan.
• Add the crushed garlic and basil and mix well.
• Add enough of the reserved tomato oil to form a thick paste around the tomatoes, season to taste and serve.

Basic mayonnaise *(makes 1¼ cups)*

Some store-bought mayonnaise is fine, but nothing can compare to a home-made version. Although taking a few minutes, making it really does pay dividends.

3 egg yolks
1 tsp Dijon mustard
1 tsp white wine vinegar
salt and freshly ground white pepper
1 cup vegetable or salad (non-scented) oil
2 tsp lemon juice

• Place the egg yolks, mustard, and vinegar in a bowl, add a little salt and pepper.
• Place the bowl on a wet cloth on a flat surface, this will help keep the bowl steady while adding the oil.
• Slowly, whisk in the oil, pouring it in a fine, steady stream from a jug or ladle.
• Whisk continuously until the mayonnaise begins to thicken; by the time all the oil has been added the mayonnaise will be thick in texture.
• Add the lemon juice and adjust the seasoning to personal taste.
• Mayonnaise will keep for 4–5 days in the refrigerator if kept covered.

PAUL GAYLER VARIATIONS
using ½ cup of the above recipe

CHUTNEY MAYO
Add ⅓ cup chopped mango chutney to the basic recipe. Great with chicken or fish burgers, such as tuna or salmon.

CURRY MAYO
Add 1 tbsp good quality curry paste to the basic recipe. Great with all types of burgers, especially chicken, pork, and lamb.

SWEET MUSTARD MAYO
Add 1 tbsp brown sugar along with the eggs, mustard, and vinegar, finish with 1 tbsp chopped fresh dill. Great with fish burgers.

AIOLI SAUCE
Add 2 large garlic cloves, crushed, to the mustard, egg, and vinegar at the beginning of the basic recipe.

SUNDRIED TOMATO AIOLI
Add 10 sundried tomatoes in oil, drained and finely chopped, to the aioli sauce. Great with all manner of burgers and for a dip for vegetables.

HORSERADISH MAYO
Add 1 tbsp freshly grated horseradish, 1 tsp Dijon mustard, along with 2 tbsp chopped fresh dill or flat-leaf parsley to the basic recipe.

WASABI MAYO
Add ¼ tsp wasabi paste (Japanese horseradish), the juice of ½ lime, and 1 tbsp light soy sauce to the basic recipe; finish with 2 tbsp chopped fresh cilantro.

OLIVE MAYO
Add 2 tbsp pitted and finely chopped black olives, 1 tsp chopped rinsed capers, and 1 small crushed garlic clove to the basic recipe.

RED OR GREEN CHILI MAYO
Add 1 tsp deseeded and very finely chopped red chili to the basic recipe and mix well. You can use green chili instead of red if you prefer.

GREEN HARISSA MAYO
Place 2 deseeded green chilies, 1 tsp toasted coriander seeds, 1 garlic clove, along with 1 cup each fresh cilantro, mint, and flat-leaf parsley, in a blender. Add ¼ cup cooked spinach and mix to a smooth purée. Add a spoonful of olive oil, if necessary. Transfer to a bowl, add the mayonnaise, and chill, ready for use.

CAPER–SAFFRON MAYO
Add ¼ tsp fresh saffron to 3 tbsp boiling water in a small pan and boil for 1 minute; remove and leave to stand for 10 minutes. Add the saffron to the mayonnaise along with 2 tbsp rinsed and chopped capers.

Red chili mayo

Beetroot and horseradish tzatziki

Chimichurri bell peppers

Salsas and relishes

Kachumbar piccalilli

Pico de gallo

Beet and horseradish tzatziki

⅛ tsp cumin seeds
4 cooked beets, peeled
½ cup Greek-style yogurt
2 tbsp chopped fresh mint
1 tbsp horseradish creamed relish
1 tsp lemon juice
salt and freshly ground black pepper

• Heat a dry frying pan over a high heat. Add the cumin seeds and toss gently for 10–20 seconds to give off their fragrance and aromatic smell. Place in a mortar and pestle and crush to a fine powder. Transfer to a bowl.
• Cut the beets into ¼-inch dice and add to the cumin. Add the remaining ingredients and season to taste.
• Cover and chill in the refrigerator for 1 hour prior to serving.

Kachumbar piccalilli

juice of 1 lime
2 tbsp tamarind paste
2 tbsp Asian sweet chili sauce
4 tbsp brown sugar
⅔ cup rice wine vinegar
1-inch piece ginger root, finely grated
1 tbsp coarse salt
¼ tsp cumin seeds, toasted
¼ tsp coriander seeds, toasted
⅛ tsp turmeric
1 tsp cornstarch
14 oz firm tomatoes, cut into wedges
4 large shallots, peeled, thickly sliced
1 cucumber, halved lengthwise, seeds removed, cut into ¼-inch sticks
2 dill pickles, thickly sliced
freshly ground black pepper

• Combine the lime juice, tamarind, chili sauce, and brown sugar in a pan, add the rice wine vinegar, mix well, and bring to a boil, simmer for 5 minutes.
• Add the ginger, salt, and spices, cook for a further 5 minutes.
• Mix the cornstarch with 2 tsp cold water, then stir into the cooking liquid, simmer for 1 minute, then add the vegetables.
• Simmer gently for 3–4 minutes or until the vegetables are tender.
• Remove to a bowl and allow to go cold, check the seasoning, and serve.

Chimichurri bell peppers

¼ cup olive oil
2 garlic cloves, crushed
1 tbsp honey
1 jalapeño chili, deseeded, finely chopped
4 large red bell peppers, deseeded, cut into large pieces
2 tbsp white wine vinegar
small bunch cilantro, roughly chopped
small bunch flat-leaf parsley, roughly chopped
1 tbsp roughly chopped fresh oregano
salt and freshly ground black pepper

• Heat the olive oil in a frying pan, add the garlic, honey, and chili, and cook over a low heat until softened and slightly caramelized.
• Add the bell-pepper pieces, cover, and cook for 5–6 minutes. Add the vinegar, cover again, and cook for a further 5 minutes.
• Remove the lid and add the herbs; increase the heat and sauté until all the liquid has evaporated, season, and serve warm.

Pico de gallo

can be made from red or yellow tomatoes

5 oz red or yellow tomatoes, deseeded, cut into ½-inch dice
4 red radishes
1 bunch scallions, finely chopped
1 yellow bell pepper, deseeded, cut into ½-inch dice
1 jalapeño chili, deseeded, thinly sliced
2 tbsp chopped fresh cilantro
juice of 2 limes
1 garlic clove, crushed

• Combine all the ingredients in a bowl, leave to marinate at room temperature for 3–4 hours to meld the flavors.
• Kept covered in the refrigerator, it will keep for a day or two, but it is better to make it as needed, when it is fresh and crisp in flavor and texture.

Cooked tomato relish

1 tbsp olive oil
2 shallots, finely chopped
1 garlic clove, crushed
1 cup brown sugar
2 tbsp white wine vinegar
1 lb ripe but firm plum tomatoes, blanched, peeled, seeded, cut into ½-inch dice
2 tbsp tomato ketchup
1 tbsp cornstarch
¼ tsp ground cumin
1 tsp Dijon mustard
salt and freshly ground black pepper

• Heat the olive oil in a pan, add the shallots and garlic, and cook for 3–4 minutes until soft but with no color. Add the sugar and vinegar, and stir in until the sugar is dissolved.
• Bring to a boil and cook for 2 minutes. Combine the tomatoes, tomato ketchup, cornstarch, and cumin, and add to the pan; reduce the heat and simmer for 15–20 minutes until thickened to a relish consistency. Remove and allow to cool before adding the mustard, and salt and pepper to taste.
• Kept well covered, this relish will keep in the refrigerator for up to 2 weeks.

PAUL GAYLER VARIATIONS

SPICY TOMATO RELISH

Add 2 small deseeded and chopped red chilies to the shallots and garlic at the beginning of the recipe (or 1 tsp harissa).

GREEK TOMATO RELISH

Add 2 tbsp Greek-style yogurt, along with 2 tbsp each chopped fresh mint and chopped fresh cilantro to the finished relish.

Calypso mojo

⅓ cup dried black beans, soaked overnight
2 tbsp frozen corn kernels, defrosted
1 small mango, peeled, cut into ½-inch dice
2 tbsp maple syrup
2 tbsp chopped fresh mint
1 tbsp olive oil
½ small red onion, thinly siced
½ garlic clove, crushed
juice of 1 lime

• Drain the beans, place in a pan, cover with water, and boil for 40–50 minutes or until soft; drain and allow to go cold.
• Place the beans in a bowl, stir in the remaining ingredients, and leave to infuse for 30 minutes before using.

Asian guacamole

2 tbsp olive oil
1 small red onion, finely shredded
½ tsp mild curry powder
2 avocados
6 scallions, finely chopped
1 hot green chili
juice of 2 limes
handful of cilantro leaves
1 tbsp sour cream

• Heat the olive oil in a pan, add the red onion, and cook for 1 minute. Add the curry powder, cook for 2 minutes, allow to go cold.
• Cut the avocados in half, remove the skins and stones.
• Place the avocados in a blender, add the remaining ingredients except the sour cream, plus the spiced onion mix. Mix into a coarse purée, then fold in the sour cream.
• Place in a bowl and refrigerate to allow the flavors to marinate for 1 hour.

Smoky tomato and bell-pepper relish

3 red bell peppers, halved, deseeded
¼ cup olive oil
1 red onion, peeled, finely chopped
2 garlic cloves, crushed
½ small red chili, deseeded, finely chopped
1 tsp smoked paprika or paprika
¼ tsp ground cumin
1 lb tomatoes, blanched, peeled, deseeded and finely chopped
1 tbsp tomato purée
2 tbsp light brown sugar
2 tbsp balsamic vinegar

• Brush the bell pepper halves with a little of the olive oil, place on a broiler pan, and place under a preheated broiler for 5–8 minutes until charred. Place in a bowl, cover tightly with plastic wrap, and leave to steam for 5 minutes; peel off the skins and finely chop the bell peppers.
• Heat 1 tbsp of the oil in a pan, add the red onion, garlic, and chili, and cook for 3–4 minutes until softened. Add the spices, cook for a further minute.
• Add the tomatoes, tomato purée, sugar, and vinegar, and bring to a boil.
• Add the bell peppers, reduce the heat, and cook for 20–25 minutes until reduced and thick in consistency.
• Remove from the heat and allow to cool; transfer to a bowl and serve cold.

Balsamic onion pickle

¾ cup dark soft brown sugar
4 large onions, finely chopped
2 Granny Smith apples, peeled, cored and chopped
½ cup balsamic vinegar
1 small red bell pepper, halved, deseeded, finely chopped
1 tsp mustard powder

• In a saucepan, place the sugar and ⅔ cup water and, over a low heat, slowly bring to a boil until the sugar dissolves.
• Add the onions, apples, balsamic vinegar, chopped bell pepper, and mustard powder, simmer gently for 1–1½ hours until the mixture becomes thick in consistency and the onions very soft and caramelized.
• Pour into a small, sterilized preserving jar, cover with waxed paper and seal. Leave for 1–2 weeks before using.

Fresh tomato salsa

6 tomatoes, deseeded, chopped
1 small red onion, peeled, chopped
1 small green chili, deseeded, finely chopped
2 tbsp freshly ground coriander
2 tbsp freshly squeezed lime juice
2 tbsp maple syrup
2 tbsp tomato ketchup (optional)
1 tsp balsamic vinegar
salt and freshly ground black pepper
• Combine all the ingredients together in a bowl, mix thoroughly, then season to taste with salt and pepper. Set aside until ready for use to let the flavors meld together.

PAUL GAYLER VARIATIONS

CORN AND CUCUMBER SALSA

Add 1 small can (7oz) corn, drained, along with ½ cup deseeded and chopped cucumber to the basic salsa recipe.

ASIAN TOMATO SALSA

Replace the red onion with 4 finely chopped scallions, plus 1-inch-piece ginger root, finely grated; replace the balsamic vinegar with rice wine vinegar. Add 1 tbsp fish sauce (nam pla).

MANGO SALSA

Add 1 pitted and chopped mango to the Asian tomato salsa variation.

CUBAN AVOCADO SALSA

Mix together 1 peeled, stoned avocado, diced, 2 tbsp chopped fresh cilantro, 1 cup diced fresh pineapple, 1 small chopped red onion, juice of 2 limes, ¼ cup olive oil, and 2 tbsp maple syrup. Leave for the flavors to meld.

GREEN TOMATO SALSA

Replace the tomatoes with green tomatoes, add 1 crushed garlic clove and a further 2 tbsp chopped fresh cilantro

Spicy cranberry–green peppercorn relish

1½ cups cranberries
⅓ cup sugar
1 Granny Smith apple, peeled, grated
½ cup orange juice
1 tsp green peppercorns, drained, rinsed
1 tbsp white wine vinegar
• Place all the ingredients in a small pan with ⅔ cup water.
• Bring to a boil slowly, then simmer until thick and of jam-like consistency. Leave to cool before use. May be kept covered in the refrigerator for up to 10 days.

Mango–coconut cream sauce

2 cups fresh cilantro leaves
⅓ cup unsweetened coconut cream
3 tbsp chopped fresh mint
2 small red chilies, deseeded, finely chopped
1-inch piece ginger root, finely grated
1 tsp freshly chopped pickled ginger
1 garlic clove, crushed
2 tbsp lime juice
2 tsp brown sugar
1 tsp ground coriander
1 mango, chopped
• Place the fresh cilantro, coconut cream, mint, chilies, gingers, garlic, lime juice, sugar, and ground coriander in a blender and mix to a smooth purée.
• Transfer to a bowl, stir in the chopped mango, and serve.

Corn and grilled pineapple mojo

vegetable or sunflower oil for cooking
2 slices fresh pineapple
¼ red bell pepper, deseeded
⅓ cup corn kernels
1 garlic clove, crushed
juice of 1 lime
2 tbsp chopped fresh mint
1 tbsp caster sugar
1 tbsp honey
salt and freshly ground black pepper
• Preheat a broiler pan to very hot, brush with a little oil. Chargrill the pineapple and bell pepper until lightly charred. Peel the bell pepper, cut in ½-inch dice. Cut the pineapple into small chunks. Place both in a bowl, add remaining ingredients, and season to taste

Tomato chutney

1¾ cups cider vinegar
1 cup sugar
3 garlic cloves, crushed
1-inch piece ginger root, peeled, finely grated
1½ tsp cayenne pepper
½ tsp ground cinnamon
3 lb 4 oz firm ripe plum tomatoes, peeled, cut into large dice
2 Granny Smith apples, peeled, cored and chopped
½ cup golden raisins
• Place the vinegar, sugar, garlic, and ginger and spices in a large pan, slowly bring the contents to a boil, stirring regularly until the sugar has dissolved.
• Lower the heat, add the tomatoes and apples, and cook over a low heat for 30 minutes to 1 hour, depending on the water content of the tomatoes. The tomatoes should remain chunky in texture.
• Add the raisins and cook for a further 10–15 minutes. Cool before use; keep refrigerated until ready for use.

Salads

Caesar salad

Coleslaw

There are as many recipes for traditional coleslaw as there are cooks who prepare it. Although coleslaw is generally made with mayonnaise, it is sometimes bound with French dressing or sour cream, which makes a welcome change.

½ white cabbage
2 carrots, peeled
1 onion, peeled
2 green bell peppers, halved, deseeded
1¼ cups good quality mayonnaise
salt and freshly ground black pepper
pinch of celery salt (optional)

• Remove the outer leaves from the cabbage, cut it into 2-inch wedges, remove and discard center core.
• Using a sharp knife, finely shred it into strips or use the shredding attachment of a food processor.
• Place the shredded cabbage in cold iced water for 30 minutes.
• Meanwhile, cut the carrots into shreds, using a knife or small kitchen mandolin. Thinly shred the onion and green bell peppers.
• Remove the cabbage from the water and drain it well. Dry it in a clean cloth.
• Place all the ingredients together in a bowl, bind with the mayonnaise, season to taste and chill until required.

PAUL GAYLER VARIATIONS

BARBECUE COLESLAW
Add 2 tbsp fresh tomato ketchup and 1 tbsp hot pepper sauce to the basic recipe.

BLUE-CHEESE COLESLAW
Replace the white cabbage with red cabbage, bind with 2 tbsp sour cream instead of mayonnaise, and add ¾ cup crumbled Roquefort cheese to the basic recipe.

RUBY SLAW
Replace the white cabbage with red cabbage, the onion with red onion. Replace the bell peppers and carrots with 2 shredded cooked beets and 2 shredded, cored red apples. Bind with French dressing and sprinkle with 2 tbsp snipped chives.

DELI COLESLAW
Replace the bell peppers with 1 tbsp shredded truffles and add 2 tbsp truffle oil to the mayonnaise base.

Celeriac rémoulade

1 celeriac, peeled, cut into matchsticks
½ cup good quality mayonnaise
2 tbsp mixed chopped fresh herbs
½ tsp Dijon mustard
⅛ tsp anchovy extract (optional)
salt and freshly ground black pepper

• Mix all the ingredients together in a bowl, season to taste.

Bacon, spinach, and red onion salad

2 tbsp olive oil
4 slices Canadian bacon
¼ cup French dressing (vinaigrette)
1½ cups young spinach leaves
1 red onion, peeled, thinly sliced

• Heat a thin film of oil in a frying pan, add the bacon and, over a high heat, cook until very crispy. Add the vinaigrette to the bacon and remove.
• Place the spinach leaves and red onion in a bowl, pour over the hot bacon vinaigrette, and toss well.

Pistachio, beet, and feta tabbouleh

1 cup cracked wheat
juice of 1 lemon
¼ cup olive oil
2 cooked beets, cut into small wedges
1 red onion, finely chopped
4 red radishes, sliced
2 tbsp chopped fresh mint
salt and freshly ground black pepper
¾ cup feta cheese, cut into ½-inch cubes
½ cup peeled pistachios

• Place the cracked wheat in a bowl, cover with boiling water and leave for 15–20 minutes; drain well and dry in a cloth. Place in a clean bowl, add the lemon juice, oil, beets, onion, radishes and mint; mix well and season to taste.
• Dress on the serving dish, scatter the feta and pistachios over before serving.

Creole rémoulade slaw

¼ cup good quality mayonnaise
1 tsp Creole mustard
1 hard-boiled egg, chopped
1 tbsp chopped fresh flat-leaf parsley
salt and freshly ground black pepper
pinch of cayenne
1 cup shredded napa cabbage (Chinese cabbage)
2 shallots, peeled, halved, thinly sliced
2 stalks celery, peeled, thinly sliced
1 red bell pepper, halved, deseeded, thinly sliced
1 anchovy fillet, rinsed, chopped

• In a bowl combine the mayonnaise with the mustard, egg, and parsley, and season to taste.
• Add the vegetables and anchovy, toss together to bind, and check the seasoning.

Caesar salad

1 egg yolk
2 garlic cloves, crushed
2 tbsp white wine vinegar
2 anchovy fillets
1 tsp Worcestershire sauce
½ tsp Dijon mustard
salt and freshly ground black pepper
1 cup light olive oil
¼ cup olive oil or melted butter
4 oz rustic country bread, cut into ½-inch dice
2 heads romaine lettuce, inner leaves only
1 cup freshly shaved Parmigiano Reggiano

• Make the dressing: place the egg yolk, garlic, vinegar, anchovies, Worcestershire sauce, mustard, and a little salt and pepper in a blender, and mix until smooth. With the motor running, gradually add the light olive oil through the feed tube.
• Heat the olive oil or butter in a frying pan, add the bread, and cook over a gentle heat until golden and crispy. Remove from the pan and allow to cool.
• Separate the romaine leaves, wash and dry them, then tear into fairly large pieces. Place in a bowl and toss with the dressing. Scatter the croutons over and sprinkle the shaved Parmesan on top.

Breads

Basic burger bun (with black sesame seeds)

Basic burger bun recipe

(makes 8)

When making these buns, I recommend using a small food processor with a dough hook, which helps aerate the mix better and gives a more satisfying result. But preparing by hand is fine.

5 cups strong bread flour
½ tsp salt
½ tsp sugar
2 tbsp unsalted butter, softened
2 tbsp fresh yeast
sunflower oil for greasing
2 tbsp plain or black sesame seeds (optional)
1 egg beaten with 1 tbsp milk

• Into a large bowl, sift the flour, salt, and sugar. Add the butter and blend well together.
• Place the yeast in a small bowl, add 1½ cups water and leave the liquid to become bubbly, about 10–15 minutes.
• Add the yeast liquid to the flour and beat well for 7–8 minutes to amalgamate the dough.
• Cover the dough with a warm damp cloth and place in a warm area for up to 1 hour to prove.
• Lightly grease a large baking tray.
• Divide the dough into 8 large balls or buns. Arrange the buns spaced well apart to allow for expansion as they cook; if using, sprinkle the sesame seeds over the surface of the buns.
• Cover again with the damp cloth, allow to prove again for 45 minutes.
• Preheat the oven to 425°F.
• Brush the top of each bun with the egg and milk glaze and place in the oven for 30–35 minutes. Remove the buns and leave to rest for 20 minutes before using.

PAUL GAYLER VARIATIONS

ONION AND THYME BUNS

Sauté 1 finely chopped onion and 1 tsp picked thyme together in 1 tbsp butter until soft, then add to the dough during the last minute of beating.

CHORIZO BUNS

Add 7 oz finely diced chorizo or bacon to the dough during the last minute of beating.

CHEESE BUNS

Add 1½ cups grated cheddar cheese, along with the butter at the beginning.

English muffins

(makes 10)

4 cups strong bread flour
1½ tsp salt
1½ tsp easy-blend dried yeast
½ tsp sugar
1 cup warm water
⅔ cup warm milk
flour for dusting

• Place the flour and salt in a large mixing bowl, add the yeast, and make a well in the center.
• Add the sugar to the lukewarm liquids and pour into the well in the flour mixture. Mix with your hands until it forms a soft and slightly sticky dough.
• Turn out the dough on to a floured work surface and knead with floured hands for 10 minutes until it is soft, elastic, smooth, and no longer sticky.
• Return the dough to the bowl, cover with a damp cloth, and leave to rise in a warm place until doubled in size, about 1 hour.
• Turn out the dough on to the work surface and knead for a further 5 minutes. Divide the dough into 10 evenly sized pieces and shape into balls. Drop onto a well-dusted baking tray, leaving plenty of room to allow for expansion, then sprinkle the balls with flour.
• Cover the tray of muffins with another lightweight baking tray and leave for 30 minutes or until doubled in size again.
• Heat a heavy cast iron frying pan or griddle until moderately hot and cook them, a few at a time, turning them as you place them on the pan. Cook them slowly for 10–12 minutes on each side, until golden brown, turning them with a palette knife during cooking. They are cooked when the surface springs back when pressed.
• Remove the muffins from the pan and leave to cool on a rack ready for use.

Pita bread

(makes 8 large or 12 mini pita breads)

These Arabic-style flatbreads are great for holding kebabs or small burgers. Ensure you have your oven set at the highest possible setting for the best result.

2 tbsp fresh yeast
pinch of sugar
1¾ cups warm water
4 cups all-purpose flour plus extra for dusting
½ tsp salt
sunflower oil for greasing

• In a bowl, mix the yeast with the sugar and 4 tbsp of the water; leave the liquid to become bubbly, about 10–15 minutes. Mix the flour and salt in a mixing bowl, make a well in the center, and add the yeast mixture. Work into a dough with the remaining water to a firm consistency. Knead for 10 minutes.
• When the dough is smooth and pliable, shape into a ball, place in a lightly greased bowl, and cover with plastic wrap or a damp cloth. Set aside in a warm place for 1–1½ hours or until doubled in size.
• Preheat the oven to 475°F or highest setting. Turn out the dough onto a floured surface. Punch down the dough, then divide into 8 or 12 equal portions. Roll each portion into a ball, dust with flour and place on a board. Cover with a dry cloth and prove for a further 15 minutes.
• Grease 3 large baking sheets lightly with oil, place in the hot oven for 5 minutes. Roll out each ball of dough on a floured surface with a floured rolling pin to a rough circle (about 6 inches diameter for large pitas). Transfer 2 or 3 at a time to a hot baking sheet. Cook in the oven for about 6 minutes until puffed up but still quite pale in color. Repeat with the remaining pitas, cooking them a few at a time.
• Place on a cooling rack, then cover with a cloth to keep them soft.

Brioche

(makes 2 loaves)

1 cup unsalted butter at room temperature
3 large eggs
2½ cups strong white bread flour
pinch of salt
1½ tsp easy-blend dried yeast
about 2 tbsp warm milk, if needed
flour for dusting
sunflower oil for greasing
1 small egg yolk, lightly beaten with 1 tsp water

• Place the butter in the bowl of a small table-top electric mixer, or mixing bowl if using a hand-held mixer. Beat until soft and creamy.
• Beat in the eggs, one at a time. Sift the flour and salt, and add to the bowl with the yeast, and beat thoroughly. If the dough seems too dry to come together, add the warmed milk. The dough should be firm at this stage.
• Fit the dough hook to the mixer, or turn out the dough on a lightly floured work surface, knead until smooth and quite elastic.
• Shape into a ball, place in a clean bowl, cover with a cloth and leave at room temperature to rise until doubled in volume.
• On a lightly floured surface, knock back the dough, then form it into an oblong shape and place on a lightly oiled loaf tin of 6-cup capacity. The dough should half fill the tin. Cover and leave to rise at room temperature until the dough fills the tin.
• Preheat the oven to 375°F.
• Brush the top of the loaf with the egg yolk mixture, then bake for about 30 minutes or until risen and golden brown.
• Test if the bread is done by tipping it out of the tin and tapping it gently on the base, it should sound hollow.
• Turn out onto a wire rack to cool.

PAUL GAYLER VARIATIONS

RICHARD CORRIGAN'S BACON BRIOCHE

• Heat a little oil in a frying pan, add 6 oz rindless bacon, cut into small pieces, and fry until golden. Add 1 finely chopped onion and 1 tsp chopped fresh marjoram, cook until softened, remove and cool.
• Add the mixture to the dough before kneading for the first time.

CHEESE BRIOCHE

Add 1 cup grated cheese to the dough before kneading for the first time.

Cumin naan bread

(makes 8 naan breads)

1 tsp cumin seeds
2¼ cups self-rising flour
2 tbsp Greek-style yogurt
1 tsp salt
½ cup warm water
½ tsp ground coriander
flour for dusting

• Heat a small pan over medium heat, add the cumin seeds, and dry toast for 20 seconds until they give off an aroma. Remove and allow to cool.
• Place the flour, yogurt, and salt in a large bowl, add the warm water, a little at a time, working it into the flour with your fingers to form a sticky dough.
• Mix in the coriander and toasted cumin seeds. Knead for a few seconds, then cover with a damp cloth to prove.
• Leave at room temperature for 1–1½ hours.
• Preheat a broiler to its highest setting.
• Flour your hands and pull off small pieces of dough, shape them into a ball.
• Roll out each ball on a floured surface to about 6–8 inches in diameter.
• Place the now-formed naans on broiling trays, place under the broiler until they puff up and blister about 50–60 seconds, turn over and repeat on the other side; serve warm.

PAUL GAYLER VARIATIONS

By adding different ingredients, you can vary this simple bread:

GARLIC NAAN

Add 2 small crushed garlic cloves to the formed dough.

MUSTARD SEED NAAN

Sprinkle the rolled naan lightly with black mustard seeds before grilling.

COCONUT NAAN

Add ⅔ cup dried desiccated coconut to the dough.

Focaccia

(makes 1 loaf)

Focaccia is an Italian-style flatbread made with good-quality olive oil. It may be made plain, as in my basic recipe below, or topped with all manner of wonderful toppings. I have included some of my particular favorites.

3 cups all-purpose flour
½ tsp salt
3 tsp easy-blend dried yeast
1 cup warm water
½ cup extra-virgin olive oil
flour for dusting
sunflower oil for greasing
1 tsp coarse sea salt

• Sift the flour and salt into a large mixing bowl, stir in the yeast, then make a well in the center of the bowl.
• Pour in the warm water and 2 tbsp of the oil, mix well, adding a little more water if the mix seems too dry in texture.
• Turn the dough out onto a lightly floured surface and knead for about 10 minutes until smooth and elastic.
• Return the dough to a greased bowl, cover with a cloth and leave in a warm place for about 1 hour until doubled in size.
• Knock back and knead the dough for 2–3 minutes.
• Preheat the oven to 425°F.
• Roll out the dough about ½ inch thick, then transfer to a greased baking sheet or small roasting tin. Cover with a cloth again and leave to rise again for 45 minutes.
• Using your fingertips, make indentations into the dough ¼ inch deep.
• Drizzle about half the remaining oil over, sprinkle the sea salt on top, and place in the oven. Bake for 25–30 minutes until golden; brush all over with the last of the olive oil, turn out onto a wire rack, and leave to cool slightly before eating.

PAUL GAYLER VARIATIONS

• Use flavored oils, such as herb, saffron or chili for an interesting change.

Top the focaccia with all manner of wonderful flavors:
• Thinly sliced red onion and chopped rosemary.
• Thinly sliced garlic and basil pesto.
• Chopped sundried tomatoes in oil, drained, and black olives.

Focaccia

Matchstick fries

Matchstick fries

2 medium-large potatoes
vegetable oil for deep frying
¼ tsp caraway seeds, toasted (optional)
½ tsp coarse sea salt

• Peel the potatoes, then using a Japanese vegetable mandolin, cut them into julienne strips.
• Wash in cold water to remove the starch.
• Dry in a clean cloth.
• Heat the oil until 350°F, add the potatoes, and fry until golden and crispy.
• Drain on kitchen paper.
• Place the caraway seeds and salt in a mortar and pestle and crush until fine, then sprinkle over the crispy fried potatoes.
• Serve hot or cold.

Oven cheese fries

2 potatoes, well washed
½ cup vegetable oil
salt and freshly ground black pepper
1 cup fresh white bread crumbs
¼ cup freshly grated cheddar cheese
¼ cup unsalted butter, melted

• Preheat the oven to 350°F.
• Cut the potatoes into thick wedges, dry well in a cloth, and place in a baking tin. Pour the vegetable oil over and toss together well. Season to taste.
• Place in the oven and cook for 25–30 minutes or until golden and crispy.
• In a bowl combine the bread crumbs, cheese, and butter, and sprinkle over the potatoes. Return the potatoes to the oven until the cheese and bread crumbs are golden and form a light golden crust on top, then serve.

Twice-cooked jacket potatoes

4 baking potatoes, well washed
¼ cup unsalted butter
2 garlic cloves
1½ cups fresh white bread crumbs
½ tsp Dijon mustard
3 tbsp chopped fresh flat-leaf parsley

• Preheat a broiler to its highest setting.
• Prick the potatoes all over with a small knife, place in a microwave for 6–8 minutes or until cooked.
• Cut the potatoes in half crosswise and stand cut-side up on a broiler pan.
• Heat a frying pan until hot, add the butter, garlic and parsley, and cook until the butter begins to foam up. Add the bread crumbs and mustard, and cook for 1 minute.
• Spoon the fried crumbs over the potatoes and place them under the broiler to broil to a golden color, remove, and serve.

The ultimate fries

4 large floury potatoes
vegetable or sunflower oil for deep frying
coarse sea salt

• Peel the potatoes, rinse under cold water, then dry in a clean cloth or kitchen paper. Cut into strips about ½ inch wide by 2–3 inches.
• Half fill a deep-fat fryer or deep, heavy based saucepan with the oil and heat it to 300°F .
• Fry the potatoes in the oil in batches for 5–8 minutes until they are soft but still very pale in color. Lift out with a slotted spoon and drain on kitchen paper. The fries can be prepared up to this stage several hours in advance, as long as the final frying is done just before serving.
• Raise the temperature of the oil to 400°F and return the fries to the oil in batches.
• Fry for 2–3 minutes until golden and crisp. Remove with a slotted spoon.
• Drain the fries on kitchen paper, then serve sprinkled liberally with the coarse salt.

PAUL GAYLER VARIATIONS

• Season the fries with a cumin and paprika salt mix, made by mixing together 1 tsp ground cumin, ¼ tsp smoked paprika or paprika, 2 tbsp coarse salt and a pinch of sugar.
• Pass the cooked fries through ¼ cup unsalted butter, melted, and mixed with 2 tbsp chopped fresh flat-leaf parsley and 2 crushed garlic cloves.
• Place the cooked fries in a dish, sprinkle with cheddar cheese, and set under a preheated hot broiler until the cheese is bubbling and golden.

Potato salad

10 oz small new potatoes, scrubbed, halved
5 tbsp vegetable oil
2 tbsp white wine vinegar
1 tsp German mustard
1 tsp caster sugar
salt and freshly ground black pepper
⅔ cup hot chicken stock
8 cherry tomatoes, halved
2 sweet dill pickled gherkins, thinly sliced
2 shallots, peeled, cut into thin rings
2 scallions, shredded
1 tbsp chopped fresh chives

• Boil the potatoes in a pan of salted water until tender, drain well, and set aside.
• In a bowl, whisk the oil, vinegar, mustard, sugar, and a little seasoning together.
• Add the chicken stock, mix together, then pour over the hot potatoes. Cover with a lid and leave to cool to room temperature, by which time the potatoes will have absorbed all the flavors.
• Transfer to a bowl and add the remaining ingredients; adjust seasoning to taste and serve (do not refrigerate or all the flavors will be lost).

Patatas con ajo

1 lb potatoes, cut into large chunks
½ cup olive oil
2 garlic cloves, crushed
salt
pinch of paprika

• Cook the potatoes in boiling, salted water until tender. Drain, saving a little of the cooking water.
• Mash the potatoes, adding a little of the reserved cooking water to make a smooth purée.
• Mix the oil, garlic, and salt, and stir into the hot mash. Serve sprinkled with a little paprika.

Vegetables

Sweet potato fries

4 large sweet potatoes
vegetable or sunflower oil for deep frying
salt and freshly ground black pepper

• Peel the sweet potatoes, rinse them, and cut into strips, lengthwise, about ½ inch thick. Pat with a clean cloth or kitchen paper to dry.
• Half fill a deep-fat fryer or deep, heavy based saucepan with the oil and heat it to 375°F.
• Fry the sweet potatoes in the oil in batches for 3–4 minutes until golden. Drain on kitchen paper, season, and serve.

Tempura sweet potatoes

2 red sweet potatoes, peeled
½ tsp ground ginger
½ tsp ground coriander
½ tsp ground cumin
small pinch of dried chili powder
1 cup all-purpose flour
salt and freshly ground black pepper
1 cup iced soda water
1 small egg white, lightly beaten
vegetable oil for deep frying

• Thinly slice the sweet potatoes on a kitchen mandolin about ¼ inch thick, place in a bowl.
• Add the spices, mix well, and leave to marinate for 1 hour.
• Whisk the flour, salt, and pepper in a bowl with the iced soda water and egg white; whisk until just blended, do not overmix. Chill for 1 hour.
• Heat a deep-fat fryer or large saucepan with sufficient oil. Working in batches, dip the potato slices into the batter, then drop into the hot oil.
• Fry until golden, remove with a slotted spoon, and drain on kitchen paper; serve hot.

Spicy red-chili onion rings

2 large onions, peeled, cut into ¼-inch-thick slices, separated into rings
½ cup buttermilk or whole milk
2 tbsp all-purpose flour
1 tbsp cornstarch
1 tbsp red chili powder
1 tsp ground cumin
1 tsp smoked paprika
½ tsp garlic powder
salt
pinch of sugar
vegetable oil for deep frying

• Place the onions in a bowl, pour the milk over, and leave to stand for 30 minutes.
• In a large bowl, mix together the flour, cornstarch, spices, and garlic powder, along with a little salt and sugar.
• Half fill a deep-fat fryer or deep, heavy based saucepan with the oil and heat it to 350°F.
• Taking a few onion rings at a time, remove them from the milk, then dip them into the flour coating.
• Fry until golden, remove and drain on kitchen paper, and serve.

Fire-roasted vegetables

2 eggplants, cut into ½-inch wedges
2 zucchini, cut into ½-inch slices
1 red bell pepper, halved, deseeded, cut into 1-inch dice
1 green bell pepper, halved, deseeded, cut into 1-inch dice
1 red onion, halved, cut into thick wedges
⅓ cup olive oil
1 garlic clove, crushed
2 tsp balsamic vinegar
salt and freshly ground black pepper
oregano leaves to garnish

• Place the cut vegetables in a large bowl.
• Mix the olive oil, garlic, and vinegar, and pour over the vegetables, season, then toss together. Leave to marinate for 1 hour.
• Thread the vegetables onto 8 pre-soaked wooden skewers, with an eye to color.
• Heat a chargrill until hot, add the skewers, and chargrill for 4–5 minutes, turning them regularly until cooked.
• Remove and serve sprinkled with oregano leaves.

Spicy plantain chips (chili willies)

2 large green plantains
vegetable oil for deep frying
coarse sea salt
large pinch of chili powder

• Green plantains can be difficult to peel—here is how you do it. Fill a sink with warm–hottish water. Cut the ends off the plantains, make 3–4 slits lengthwise through the skin, then leave to soak in the water for 20–25 minutes. Once soaked, you can easily peel them by running your fingers under the skin. Slice the plantains ⅛ inch thick.
• Half fill a deep-fat fryer or deep, heavy based saucepan with the oil and heat it to 350°F.
• Drop the plantain slices, a few at a time, into the oil. and fry until golden and crisp. Drain on kitchen paper; season with salt and a touch of chili powder, toss gently, and serve.

Chickpea fries

2½ cups chickpea flour (gram flour)
1 garlic clove, crushed
salt and freshly ground black pepper
olive oil for greasing
vegetable oil for deep frying

• Place the chickpea flour and garlic in a pan with a little salt and pepper. Whisk in 3 cups water to form a smooth paste.
• Place on a low–medium heat, whisking continuously until very thick, about 5 minutes. Then beat with a wooden spoon until completely smooth.
• Lightly grease a small loaf tin with the olive oil. Transfer the chickpea mix into the tin and smooth off the surface with a wet knife.
• Cover the tin with foil and place in the refrigerator overnight.
• Unmold the terrine onto a cutting board, then cut into ½-inch-thick slices, then cut each slice into ¼-inch strips to form thin fries.
• Half fill a deep-fat fryer or deep, heavy based saucepan with the oil and heat it to 350°F.
• Working in small batches, cook the fries until golden.
• Remove with a slotted spoon onto kitchen paper, lightly season with salt, and serve.

Spicy plantain chips (chili willies)

Index

Acknowledgments

Author

I gratefully thank and acknowledge the assistance of the following people, wonderful individuals, without whose support this book would not have been possible.
To Jacqui and Kate at Jacqui Small Publishers for inspiring me to write this book, thank you for your friendship and encouragement.
Linda Tubby, Gus Filgate and Lawrence Morton for their individual artistic skills.
Madeline Weston and Jane Middleton who helped turn my aspirations into print.
My personal assistant Lara King for just organizing me!
Ryan Stevenson, my assistant pastry chef, for never complaining when I asked for yet another batch of buns, breads or focaccia for photo shoots ... great job, and Danilo Sita for helping with the recipe preparation. To all my family, and my agents, for their continued support and enthusiasm with my writing.

Guest Recipes

I would like to thank the following select chefs, writers and friends, for whom I hold the utmost admiration, for graciously supplying their favorite burger recipes for inclusion in this book (in order of appearance):
Mark McEwan, Eula Mae Doré, Chris Galvin, Richard Corrigan, Anthony Worrall Thompson, Jill Dupleix, Andrew Blake, Marcus Samuelsson, Peter Gordon.